International Finger Food

A Nibbler's Tour of 10 Flavorful Cuisines

Amy Texido and Carol Taylor
Illustrated by Kate Brennan Hall

Lark Books

Dedication

In the course of writing and illustrating this book, each of us lost someone with whom we had shared many a good meal and many a good time. In gratitude for all the laughter and sustenance, we dedicate this book to the memories of Damian Grismer, William Taylor, and Marie Brennan.

—Amy Texido, Carol Taylor, Kate Brennan Hall

Art Director: Dana Irwin
Production: Elaine Thompson and Dana Irwin

Library of Congress Cataloging-in-Publication Data
Texido, Amy.
    International finger food : a nibbler's tour of 10 flavorful cuisines /
Amy Texido and Carol Taylor : illustrations by Kate Brennan Hall.
        p.   cm.
    Includes bibliographical references and index.
    ISBN 0-937274-77-1 : $18.95
    1. Appetizers.   2. Cookery, International.   I. Taylor, Carol.
II. Title
TX740.T415   1994
641.8'12--dc20   94-18477
                                                 CIP

10 9 8 7 6 5 4 3 2 1

Published by Lark Books
50 College St.
Asheville, NC 28801

Copyright © 1994, Lark Books

Distributed in Canada by Sterling Publishing,
    c/o Canadian Manda Group, P.O. Box 920, Station U, Toronto,
    Ontario, Canada M8Z 5P9
Distributed in Great Britain and Europe by Cassell PLC, Villiers House,
    41/47 Strand, London WC2N 5JE, England
Distributed in Australia by Capricorn Link (Australia) Pty Ltd., P.O.Box 6651,
    Baulkham Hills, Business Centre, NSW 2153, Australia

Printed in Hong Kong
All rights reserved

ISBN 0-937274-77-1

C O N T E N T S

Welcome to International Finger Food!

The love of good food is as universal as the love of good weather. Although the definition of "good" (and even of "food") varies widely from culture to culture, people everywhere seem to take enormous pleasure in eating well and in cooking for their family and friends. It's a rare celebration that doesn't involve a snack or two.

We'd like to join the party. In this book, we're not concerned with everyday, what-am-I-going-to-have-for-dinner cooking. Rather, we have focused on cooking as a hobby, on food as fun.

Nor have we paid much attention to this week's dogma of what's good for you and what isn't. Instead, we've included recipes that have stood the test of decades and even centuries—finger foods so characteristic of a given country that any citizen would recognize them.

Why International?

With the possible exception of the British empire, there's one good thing to be said for the conquest of one society by another: The food gets better.

Consider an example. When Moors from North Africa invaded Spain in 711, they brought with them almonds, lemons, oranges, and saffron—all previously unknown to Europe, all defining ingredients of modern Spanish cuisine. When Spain invaded Central America eight centuries later, they brought along hogs and citrus trees; now pork, lemons, and limes are essential elements of Mexican and Caribbean food. When the Spanish conquistadors returned to Europe, they transported back across the Atlantic such exotic American natives as tomatoes, peppers, and potatoes. All are now central to European cooking.

In short, human beings have traded recipes for centuries—often peacefully, often not—and eaten better and more adventurously because they did. When you're tired of everything you've ever cooked (and most of what you've eaten), kitchen travel is a splendid antidote to boredom.

Exploring the food of another culture is much like hiking a mile in someone else's boots: Both instill a strong sense of kinship with the rightful owner. After a weekend of cooking Thai or Mexican or Moroccan, the geography, the politics, and the general well-being of the host country become extraordinarily interesting.

Why Finger Foods?

Everybody likes to snack. Nibbles are known as *mezedes* in Greece, *antojitos* in Mexico, *hors d'oeuvres* in France, *antipasti* in Italy, *tapas* in Spain. Almost universally, small bites are used before meals to whet the appetite and between meals to subdue it.

Almost everybody likes to eat with their hands. Cultures vary in how broadly they define "finger food"—how messy the food (and the diner) can get before etiquette demands an implement or two.

There are some foods that people agree, almost unanimously, are finger foods. Nuts—plain, roasted, or deep-fried—appear everywhere. If a country has a coastline and an ocean populated with shellfish, shrimp are invariably finger food. (Perhaps it's the handy little tails.) Other universals include battered and deep-fried vegetables (Japanese *tempura*, Indian *pakoras*); small, stuffed pastries (Indian *samosas*, Mexican *empanadas*, Greek *tyropittakia*); and meatballs (Indian *kebabs*, Greek *keftedes*).

The Recipes

For all their commonality, each culture prepares a dish in its own distinctive way. In finding, selecting, and modifying recipes for this book, we have kept the ingredients and techniques as authentic as possible. When an ingredient seems almost impossible to find without a plane ticket, we've suggested a substitute. We've also provided a few hints for tracking down the obscure ones (see "Finding Exotic Ingredients" on page 42.)

Nifty Equipment

While not essential, a few lesser-known tools are so useful that they deserve special mention.

Mortar and pestle. These ancient tools are still valuable. In some cuisines—Thai, Mexican, and Indian, for example—a mortar and pestle help produce an authentic texture and taste that a blender or food processor can't. Besides, a mortar and pestle look exotic and feel adventurous.

Spice grinder. Light years separate the taste of canned, ground cardamom, coriander, cloves, cumin, and even cinnamon from the freshly ground variety. A grinder is an excellent investment, especially for spice-driven cuisines, such as India's. A coffee grinder will do fine. The spices won't be as finely ground, but a little extra texture won't do any harm. Just be sure to wash the grinder before the next pot of coffee.

Herb Chopper. This inexpensive hand tool is a great time saver. It consists of a series of sharp, metal wheels held parallel to each other in a wooden or plastic frame. To use it, grasp the handle and roll it back and forth over the herbs.

Kitchen scale. Different cultures measure ingredients differently. Flour, for example, is measured by volume in one country and by weight in another. A small, inexpensive scale marked in both ounces and grams is invaluable for weight-based measurements.

Comfortable stools. Most of the time, sociable cooking is more fun than solitary cooking. Give your friends and family places to sit. (As long as they're in the neighborhood, they might as well chop the cilantro.)

Encouraging Words

No matter how unnerving they look, taste new ingredients. If you don't know what tamarind or lemon grass or fish sauce actually tastes like, you won't know when a dish has too much or too little of it, and you won't be able to adjust the seasoning to your liking. It's a heady moment when you first improvise in another cuisine—which you can do if you know that tamarind is sour, lemon grass is citrusy, and fish sauce is salty.

Bon voyage!

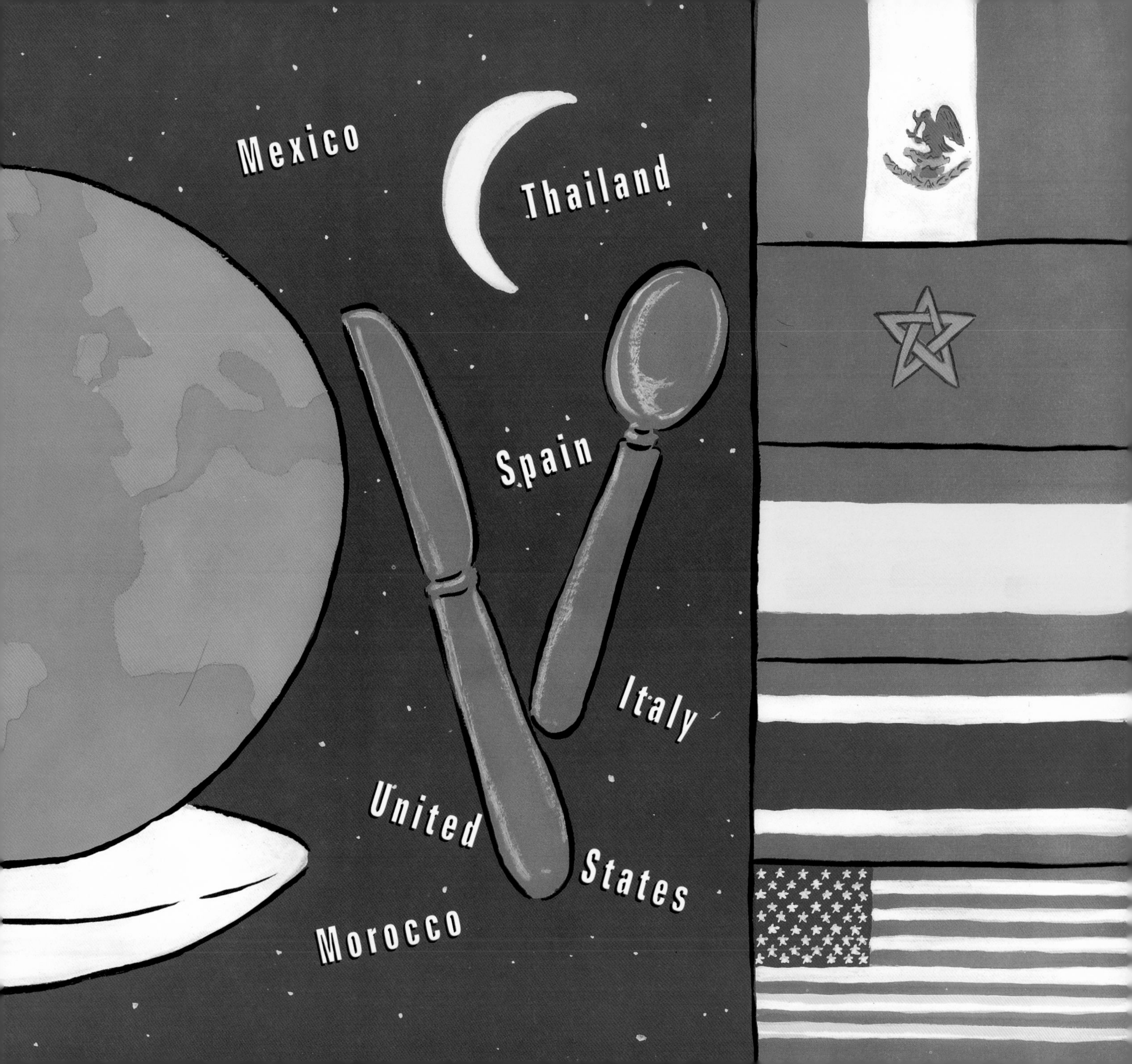
Mexico
Thailand
Spain
Italy
United States
Morocco

Mexico

Defining Ingredients

Corn (masa harina, cornmeal), beans, tomatoes, fresh cheese, cumin, chilies, cilantro, lime, cinnamon, chocolate

With the possible exception of military invasions, rarely has one culture exported its cuisine as widely and as decisively as Mexico has. During the 1980s and '90s, salsas, tacos, and enchiladas appeared on dinner tables and in street stands from New York to London to Amsterdam. It's a rare food lover who requires a translation of "quesadilla" or "guacamole."

Mexico's conquest of international eating has been a peaceful one, accomplished with the consent of the governed. The heat of chilies…the silky smoothness of avocados…the crunch of cornmeal…the mellow tastes and colors of the much undervalued "common" bean—they have made collaborators of us all.

The last time Mexico exported its food to the rest of the world was not so pacific an event. In the 16th century the Spanish conquistadors arrived in Mexico, seeking a route to the Spice Islands. They found instead a high civilization with a well-developed system of agriculture and a wealth of native foods unknown in Europe. The conquerors carried the new foods back to Spain and thence to the rest of Europe, Asia, and Northern Africa.

TORTILLAS

∎

The national bread of Mexico, tortillas are thin, flat, and pliable. Most are made of corn, the national grain, but flour ones are popular in the northern part of the country.

Tortillas are excellent utensils that turn almost anything into finger food. Tear off a piece, fold it to make it stronger, and scoop up whatever morsel is available.

Tortillas freeze well; just place them in airtight plastic bags. After a couple of weeks in the refrigerator, they lose much of their flavor and become stiff and dry. To soften them, cover them with a damp paper towel and microwave for 30 seconds. Steaming also softens and moistens them. Wrap a stack of tortillas in a dish towel, place them in a steamer over water, cover, and bring to a boil. When steam forms, cook 1 minute. Remove from the heat and let stand for 5 minutes.

Here is a partial list of the food that the New World gave the Old: corn, potatoes, tomatoes, beans, pumpkins, squash, peppers, chocolate, avocados, sweet potatoes, and pineapples. Although some of these foods are now intimately identified with other countries (Italy without tomatoes is unthinkable), all were originally gifts from Mexico.

Techniques are simple in Mexican cooking; the character of the dish results more from the ingredients than from any complex procedure. As a result, most dishes are infinitely adaptable to individual tastes. Salsas—the wonderful fresh and cooked sauces that can turn plain beans or broiled meat into memorable fare—are perfect examples. Although the ingredients are fairly standard, the relative amounts vary with every cook in Mexico—which leaves the rest of us free to add more of anything we like.

Pepitas

Toasted pumpkin seeds are among the most common Mexican snacks. They can be purchased in bulk at health food stores or rescued from a fresh pumpkin.

To prepare fresh seeds, remove all the flesh, rinse them, and spread them on clean newspaper to dry. To toast the seeds, spread them in a single layer on a baking sheet. Bake at 350°F until crisp and lightly browned, about 5 to 10 minutes.

Pico de Gallo

"Beak of the rooster," the name translates, presumably because of the small bits of food that compose this fresh sauce. (Say "PEE-co de GAH-yo" and you'll be close.) The finer the dice, the more the flavors will blend.

2 large, ripe tomatoes, cored and finely chopped
1 jalapeño pepper, finely chopped
1/2 small onion, finely chopped
1 clove garlic, minced

2 to 3 tablespoons finely chopped cilantro
Salt to taste
2 to 3 teaspoons fresh lime juice

Combine the first five ingredients, add salt to taste, and stir in the lime juice. Let stand, refrigerated, for an hour or more. Taste the salsa and adjust it to your liking.

NOTE: The salsa may be too sharply acid if the tomatoes aren't sweet. If so, you might add a teaspoon of sugar, not to sweeten but to cut the acidity.

Prep time: 20 minutes
Yield: 1-1/2 cups

Salsa Verde

This "sauce green" is made from tomatillos—small, green, tomato-like vegetables with brown, papery husks.

1/2 pound (about 6 to 10, depending on size)
fresh tomatillos or one 13-ounce can
2 serrano or 1 jalapeño pepper, chopped
1/2 small onion, chopped
5 or 6 sprigs cilantro, chopped
Salt

If using fresh tomatillos, remove the husks and rinse the tomatillos. Simmer in water to cover until softened but not mushy, about 5 minutes. If using canned tomatillos, simply drain them.

Place everything but the salt in a blender or food processor, and process until you have a coarse puree. Pour into a serving dish and stir in enough water to make a medium-thick consistency. Add salt to taste, and let stand an hour before serving.

Prep time: 30 minutes
Yield: 1-1/2 cups

CORN

To Native Americans, corn was the great "mother and nourisher," the "giver of life." A Central American native domesticated at least 5,000 years ago, this giant grass fed Aztec and Maya, Inca and Iroquois, Navaho and Zuni alike.

Corn was able to support several high civilizations because of the way it was grown, cooked, and eaten. Columbus, who had departed a Europe where seed was haphazardly broadcast and allowed to grow up with the weeds, marveled at the neatness and economy of Indian agriculture. Without benefit of draft animals, fields were divided with geometric precision; in the center of each square, a mound was planted with corn, winter squash, and beans. The beans grew up the tall, straight corn-stalks for support, and the sprawling squash vines crowded out the weeds. The vegetables were also eaten together, and that was vital. Although corn is about 10% protein, it is deficient in two of the essential amino acids: lysine and tryptophan. Beans, rich in both, completed the protein, and squash supplied vitamin A.

Cooking was equally important. Universally, Native Americans added a pinch of ashes—hardwood or burned mussel shells—to a pot of corn. While corn contains niacin, a crucial B vitamin, it is bound up with another molecule, which makes it unavailable to humans. Ash—lime, or alkali—unbinds the niacin and makes it usable. Wherever corn has become the primary staple of a culture without the dietary traditions that went with it, disease and death have followed: pella-gra in Europe, Africa, and

14

Picadillo Empanadas

Empanadas—spicy little turnovers—are among the most common street food sold by vendors all over Mexico. These are stuffed with a spicy ground meat mixture. (*Picadillo* means "hash.")

For the dough:

2-1/2 teaspoons dry active yeast
1/2 tablespoon sugar
1/2 cup milk (divided)
1 egg, lightly beaten
1 large egg yolk, lightly beaten
1/3 cup sour cream

5 tablespoons unsalted butter,
   melted and cooled
2-1/2 cups all-purpose flour
1-1/4 cups yellow cornmeal
3/4 teaspoon salt

For the filling:

1-1/4 cups finely chopped onion
2 teaspoons minced garlic
2 jalapeño peppers, minced
2 teaspoons ground cumin
1 tablespoon chili powder
1 tablespoon dried oregano
1/2 teaspoon cinnamon
1/8 teaspoon ground cloves
2 tablespoons vegetable oil

1 pound ground chuck
1/4 cup tomato paste
28-ounce can plum tomatoes
   including the juice, chopped
1/3 cup raisins
1/2 cup pimento-stuffed green olives,
   chopped
Dried hot red pepper flakes to taste
Salt and freshly ground pepper to taste

To make the dough:

In a large mixing bowl, place the yeast, sugar, and 1/4 cup of the milk. Allow to stand for 5 minutes, or until the mixture is foamy. Beat in the remaining milk, egg, egg yolk, sour cream, and butter.

In another bowl, stir together the flour, cornmeal, and salt. With an electric mixer set on low, gradually beat the flour mixture into the egg-and-milk mixture until the dough is smooth and elastic.

Form the dough into a ball. Transfer to an oiled bowl, and turn to coat with the oil. Cover and let rise in a warm place for 1-1/2 hours. Punch down.

To make the filling:

In a heavy skillet, cook the onion, garlic, jalapeños, cumin, chili powder, oregano, cinnamon, cloves, and pepper in the oil over low heat until the onion is soft. Add the ground chuck and cook over moderately high heat until the meat is no longer pink. Stir to break up any lumps.

Add the tomato paste, tomatoes with juice, raisins, olives, red pepper flakes, and salt and pepper to taste. Simmer the mixture for 15 minutes, stirring occasionally, until most of the liquid has evaporated. Allow to cool.

Assembly and cooking:

Preheat oven to 450°F.

Divide the dough into 24 pieces and shape into balls. Keep dough covered with damp cloth.

On a lightly floured surface, roll each piece of dough into a 4-inch round. Use a cookie cutter to trim the edges.

Place a scant 1/4 cup of filling on the bottom two-thirds of each round and fold the rounds in half, enclosing the filling. Seal the edges of the dough and crimp decoratively.

Transfer the empanadas with a spatula to a lightly oiled baking sheet and bake them in the middle of the oven for 10 to 15 minutes, or until golden. Transfer to a cooling rack and cool before serving.

Prep time: 1 hour 30 minutes
Yield: 24 empanadas

Sopes

These little corn cups are our adaptation of the Mexican masa boats—small containers that can hold any tasty filling you like. Tradition calls for the use of *masa harina*—coarse, dry corn flour—which requires additional soaking time. We've used readily available cornmeal to eliminate extra steps. Select the fillings for a variety of colors and textures.

the southern United States; kwashiorkor in Africa. (*Kwashiorkor* means "disease of the older child when a sibling is born." It occurs when a child is weaned and placed on a corn-based diet.)

When European colonists arrived in Massachusetts in November of 1620 with nothing but some moldy wheat seeds, they managed to keep half their number alive by digging up (and recognizing as food) several caches of corn the Indians had buried for winter storage. Squanto, an amiable Indian who must have anticipated further losses ("there goes the neighborhood"), taught the colonists to plant and harvest their own maize. The next year, they made good the purloined grain.

Tortillas, cornbread, hoe cake, johnnycake— Americans have been corn fed since pre-Columbian times.

AVOCADOS

∎

Indigenous to Mexico, avocados are inexpensive in most regions of Mexico and commonplace on the table. Their subtle flavor and luxurious texture are splendid additions to most dishes. Prepare avocados at the last moment, because the peeled flesh darkens rapidly. Unfortunately, the notion that adding lemon or lime juice will retard the darkening is an old chef's tale. Leaving the pit in the unused part of the fruit may help—at least, according to young chefs.

4 ounces cream cheese, softened
6 ounces unsalted butter, softened
1 cup yellow cornmeal

2 cups all-purpose flour
1/4 teaspoon salt

Preheat oven to 350°F.

With an electric mixer, cream together the cream cheese and butter.

Sift together the cornmeal, flour, and salt. A little at a time, add the flour mixture to the cheese mixture. Stir until well incorporated. Knead 3 minutes.

Divide the dough into 60 balls and flatten them into rounds approximately 1 inch in diameter. Place each round into a mini muffin cup, pressing down to form a cup.

Bake corn cups about 20 minutes, or until lightly golden. When done, allow to cool completely before removing from pan and filling.

Fillings:

Guacamole, Black Bean and Corn Salsa, Pico de Gallo, Carnitas with Salsa Verde (see recipes in this chapter)

Prep time: 1 hour
Yield: 60 cups

Guacamole

Look for the bumpy, black-skinned Haas avocados, which have more flavor than the smooth-skinned, green variety. If you like extra heat in your guacamole, add a few drops of Tabasco sauce. If you're using guacamole as a cooling contrast to other hot Mexican food, omit the Tabasco.

2 large, ripe Haas avocados, peeled and pitted
1 tomato, seeded and chopped fine
2 tablespoons chopped onion
1 jalapeño pepper, minced

2 cloves garlic, minced
Salt and freshly ground pepper
Juice of 2 limes

In a large bowl, mash the avocados with a fork or potato masher. The mixture should be fairly smooth, but a few lumps add character.

Stir in the remaining ingredients and mix well.

To store guacamole, cover it with plastic wrap, placing the wrap directly on the surface, to keep out the air and reduce discoloration, and refrigerate. Serve at room temperature within 2 hours of preparing.

Prep time: 20 minutes
Yield: about 1-1/2 cups

Jicama and Orange

Jicama ("HEE-kah-mah") is often called a "Mexican potato" by gringos because of its brown skin and crisp, white flesh. The taste, however, is quite different. Its clean, slightly sweet taste balances spicy or heavy flavors. Peeled and sliced into rounds, sticks, or wedges, it is superb with dips.

Juice of 1 lime, freshly squeezed
2 tablespoons sugar
1 teaspoon ground medium-hot red chili pepper
   or hot paprika
Pinch salt
1 medium jicama, peeled and sliced thin
2 oranges, peeled and sliced thin

Place the lime juice in a bowl. In another bowl, combine the sugar, ground chili, and salt.

Dip jicama and orange wedges in lime juice, then lightly coat them with the sugar-and-pepper mixture. Serve quickly, before the fruit sweats and sheds its topping.

NOTE: Do not use cayenne pepper. Rather than adding an enjoyable heat to the vegetables, it will cauterize your mouth for the rest of the day. Note, also, that sliced ripe mangos are excellent replacements for the orange slices.

SANGRIA

∎

Soda pop and beer are the most common drinks with a Mexican dinner, but sangria is also a popular spirit warmer. To make the simplest and most traditional version, combine 2/3 cup fresh lime juice, 2/3 cup sugar, 3 cups red wine, and 1 cup sparkling water. Garnish with slices of lime.

Prep time: 15 minutes
Yield: 4 to 6 servings

Carnitas con Salsa

Slow-roasted pork served with spicy salsa is a popular Mexican dish.

2 pounds pork shoulder	*1/4 cup minced cilantro*
1 tablespoon onion powder	*1/4 cup chopped parsley*
Salt and black pepper to taste	*Salsa verde (see recipe on page 13)*

Preheat oven to 200°F.

Cut pork shoulder into bite-size pieces, about 1 inch square. Place the pork in a shallow roasting pan or jellyroll pan and sprinkle with onion powder, salt, and pepper, tossing to coat. Bake for 2 hours.

Remove pork from oven and sprinkle with chopped cilantro and parsley. Serve with toothpicks and dipping salsa.

Prep time: 10 minutes
Cooking time: 2 hours
Yield: 8 servings

Black Bean and Corn Salsa

A substantial, delicious addition to quesadillas.

16-ounce can black beans, rinsed and drained	*1 tablespoon red wine vinegar*
3/4 cup corn kernels, fresh or frozen and thawed	*3 tablespoons vegetable oil*
2 medium plum tomatoes, seeded and chopped	*2 tablespoons minced cilantro*

4 scallions, sliced thin

1/2 teaspoon ground cumin

Salt and black pepper to taste

Combine all ingredients. Allow to stand for 1/2 hour before serving.

Prep time: 20 minutes
Yield: about 3 cups

Drunken Oysters

Although the oysters are tipsy from white wine and a dizzying collection of herbs, the dish is quite mild.

24 fresh oysters
1/3 cup freshly squeezed lime juice
1/3 cup freshly squeezed lemon juice
2 tablespoons orange juice
1 clove garlic, crushed
1/4 teaspoon dried marjoram
1/2 teaspoon dried oregano

1 bay leaf
Freshly ground black pepper to taste
1/4 cup vegetable oil
1/3 cup dry white wine
2 serrano peppers, finely chopped
1 small onion, finely chopped
2 tablespoons chopped cilantro

Remove the oysters from their shells and set aside. Wash half the shells and reserve.

Place citrus juices and herbs in a small saucepan and bring to a boil. Immediately remove mixture from the heat and allow to cool.

Heat the oil in a skillet and sauté oysters very lightly—about 3 minutes. Drain the oysters on paper towels.

Combine wine, chilies, and onion in a large bowl. Add the citrus-herb mixture and the oysters, and stir to coat. Cover and refrigerate for 3 hours or overnight.

To serve, spoon the oysters into the reserved shells and spoon sauce over them. Sprinkle with chopped cilantro.

Prep and cooking time: 40 minutes
Marinating time: 3 hours
Yield: 6 servings

LIMES

The Mexican lime is the yellow Key lime of southern Florida: smaller and tarter, with less juice, than the bright green Persian lime known to much of the world. If a recipe from a cookbook written in Mexico calls for "the juice of one lime," it's wise to add less if you're cooking with Persian limes, in case the original reference was to the Mexican variety. You can always add more juice if you need to.

Packages of dried cornhusks are available in Mexican markets and in many well-stocked groceries. If you can't find any, you can dry your own. Pull the husks from a few ears of fresh corn, being careful not to tear them. Remove any clinging silk from the husks and rinse them well. Arrange them in a single layer on clean newspapers and allow them to dry for about a week. Store in an airtight container for future use.

Green Corn Tamales

Tamales are party food—savory morsels of cornbread, cheese, and chilies wrapped in cornhusks and steamed. Since they're fun to prepare, there's often a tamale-making party before the actual get-together takes place.

2 cups corn kernels, fresh or frozen and thawed
3 cups yellow cornmeal (divided)
1/4 cup vegetable shortening
1/4 cup unsalted butter
1/4 cup plus 2 tablespoons sugar
1/4 cup half-and-half

1-1/2 teaspoons salt
6 ounces cheddar cheese, cut into strips
2 7-ounce cans whole mild green chilies,
    cut into strips
1 package dry cornhusks

The filling:

In a food processor, grind the corn with 1-1/2 cups of the cornmeal to a chunky purée. Do not overprocess.

In a large mixing bowl, beat the shortening and butter until creamy, using an electric mixer. In another bowl, combine the sugar, half-and-half, and salt. Add to the butter mixture. Stir in the corn purée and the remaining cornmeal and mix well.

Assembly and cooking:

Soften the dried cornhusks by blanching for about 1 minute. Drain in a colander and pat dry.

Tear a few extra husks into strips about 7 inches long and 1/4 inch wide.

Lay a large cornhusk on the work surface, with the pointed end facing toward you. Spread 2 tablespoons of the filling down the center of the husk and flatten it somewhat. You'll need a border of 1-1/2 inches of uncovered husk at the bottom and about 1 inch on each side. Place a strip of cheese and a strip of chili down the center of the filling. Top with another 2 tablespoons of filling. Press to seal the filling around the cheese and chilies.

Fold the long sides of the husk over the filling. Fold up the tapered end of the husk to form a tightly closed bottom. Tie the tamale around the middle with the cornhusk strips or with string. Don't tie them too tightly or stand them too close together in the steamer; they need room to expand. Repeat with the remaining husks.

Stand tamales, bottom down, in a steamer rack and place rack over boiling water. Cover and steam until tamales are firm to the touch, at least 45 minutes. To test for doneness, remove a tamale from the center and open it. It should be firm and the corn mixture should pull away from husk easily. Tamales should not have a raw taste or doughy texture.

NOTE: There are lots of ways to fold tamales. If you don't like the method we've described, try using less filling, or laying two husks side by side, or folding over both top and bottom. If you can wrap Christmas presents, you can make a tamale.

If cornhusks are unavailable, you can use banana leaves, parchment paper, or, as a last resort, aluminum foil cut to size.

Tamales can be prepared and cooked up to 3 days in advance and stored in the refrigerator, tightly covered. To serve, re-steam about 20 minutes.

Prep time: 1 hour 15 minutes
Yield: 24 tamales

Spinach Quesadillas

8 flour tortillas
16 to 24 fresh spinach leaves, washed and dried
2 cups grated Monterey jack cheese

2 jalapeño peppers, chopped
Vegetable oil for frying

Lay 4 tortillas on the work surface. Top each tortilla with 4 to 6 spinach leaves, 1/2 cup grated cheese, and 1/2 chopped jalapeño. Cover with a second tortilla.

Cover the bottom of a frying pan with vegetable oil and heat over medium heat. Fry the quesadillas, turning once, until cheese is melted and tortillas are slightly crisp. To serve, cut each quesadilla into four wedges.

Serve with Black Bean and Corn Salsa (see page 18).

Prep and cooking time: 30 minutes
Yield: 4 to 6 servings

BOUNTIFUL BEANS

As the homeland of the common bean (Phaseolus vulgaris), Mexico is the original source of one of the world's best and most important foods, the major form of nonvegetable protein worldwide. The ancestral bean came under cultivation 7,000 years ago in southwestern Mexico. Native Americans carried it north and south in the Western Hemisphere, and Spanish explorers transported it back to Europe.

That original bean has developed into literally hundreds of varieties, including such standbys as navy, field, kidney, pinto, and black beans. Today, as many as 30 different kinds can be found for sale in Mexican markets.

21

Greece and the Middle East

Defining Ingredients

Olives, olive oil, chick-peas, lemons, eggplant, phyllo, feta, grape leaves, yogurt, garlic, bell peppers, tomatoes, oregano, thyme, mint, dill, honey

Despite the substantial differences—cultural, political, and religious—between Greece and Middle Eastern countries, there are striking similarities in the food. They rely on many of the same ingredients and share a number of virtually identical dishes. Stuffed grape leaves, perhaps Greece's most famous dish, are served all over the Middle East. Baba ghanoush, the seductive Middle Eastern eggplant puree, is close kin to the Greek *melitzanosalata*. Garlicky mayonnaise, yogurt dips enriched with walnuts, miniature meatballs—all appear on meze tables throughout the region. (Originally a Persian word, *meze* means appetizer or snack in both Greece and the Middle East.)

Greek and Middle Eastern approaches to food are similar. Both cuisines are intimately related to the seasons; what is on

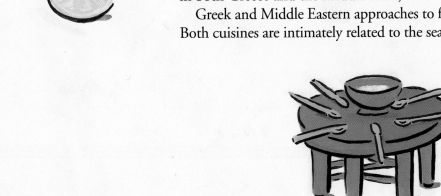

OLIVES AND THEIR OIL

According to Greek mythology, the god Poseidon and the goddess Athena staged a contest: Who could give humanity a more valuable present? Poseidon's gift was the horse; Athena's was the olive tree.

Athena won.

Native to the eastern Mediterranean, olives have been cultivated since at least 3,000 B.C. Today, virtually all of the world's olive acreage is Mediterranean, with 90% of the crop used for oil. And that's barely enough. It takes 1,500 to 2,000 olives to make one quart of oil.

Olive oil is graded according to how it's extracted from the olives. Virgin oil

the table depends upon what is fresh from the garden or market. Both cuisines are painted in broad strokes. In most dishes there are a few bold, instantly identifiable flavors. There is a shared presumption that the character of the ingredients should shine through the finished dish undisguised.

Add the traditions of hospitality, conviviality, and gusto that accompany the consumption of food in both Greece and the Middle East, and you have a shared tradition of good food and good company.

There are three basic types of mezedes: hot or cooked snacks; dips and spreads; and salads, pickles, and vegetables. A good meze table, with a sampling of each, is a fine place to join family or friends, to rehash the day, unwind, and revel in good food.

Tzatziki

This cucumber-and-yogurt dip is likely to appear on any meze table in Greece, whether at home, in a tavern, or in a restaurant. It's cooling and delicious with toasted pieces of pita bread and a good accompaniment to Greek meatballs (see recipe on page 26).

2 medium cucumbers
1 tablespoon minced garlic
2 tablespoons olive oil
2 tablespoons finely chopped dill
1-1/2 tablespoons white vinegar
Salt and pepper to taste
1-1/4 to 1-1/2 cups yogurt cheese
  (see "Yogurt" on page 97)

Peel, seed, and coarsely grate the cucumbers. Squeeze out all the moisture you can. Stir the grated cucumbers and remaining ingredients into the yogurt cheese and allow to stand an hour.

Prep time: 20 minutes
Yield: about 2 cups

Feta and Walnut Dip

One of Greece's most famous foods is salty, pungent feta cheese. This intensely flavored dip is good with crackers, pita triangles, or fresh vegetables. Most groceries carry feta in the deli sections.

1/2 pound feta
2 tablespoons olive oil
2/3 cup milk
1 cup walnuts
Dash cayenne
2 tablespoons minced parsley

Drain the feta. Combine all ingredients in a food processor and process until smooth. (Because of the walnuts, the dip will be somewhat grainy.) Let stand 1 hour before serving.

Prep time: 15 minutes
Yield: 2 cups

comes from the first, or "cold," pressing. Free of impurities, it is unrefined and thus purest in flavor. Subsequent pressings involve heat and thus extract components that give the oil a bitter flavor, requiring that it be refined to restore the taste.

Raw olives fresh from the tree are inedible; they contain a bitter substance that must be removed in some way. The Romans accomplished this by soaking the olives in lye—still standard procedure everywhere but Greece, where olives are simply soaked in water and then in brine. Greek olives are especially strong-flavored.

Olives are usually harvested in the fall and considered cured by early spring. They are then packed in either fresh brine, brine and vinegar, olive oil, or olive oil and vinegar.

OLIVES: A USER'S GUIDE

Kalamata. *The most famous Greek variety. A splendid olive, large and almond-shaped. Part of its flavor comes from the red-wine vinegar used in the curing. Named for the town of Kalamata.*

Greek black olive. *Brine-cured, meaty, and plump, often sold in bulk bins in delis. The basis for California black olives.*

Alfonso. *An Italian olive. Large, black, and delicious.*

Royal. *Huge Greek black olives cured in olive oil.*

Gaeta. *Small, black, smooth Italian olives, often packed in oil and herbs.*

Miniature Meatballs

Meatballs can be served with toothpick "skewers" or pita bread "scoops."

1-1/2 pounds ground lamb or beef, or a combination of the two
1 large red onion, finely chopped
1/4 cup finely chopped parsley
1-1/2 teaspoons dried oregano
1 teaspoon dried thyme
1 tablespoon prepared brown mustard
1/4 cup dry red wine
2 tablespoons red wine vinegar
1 cup bread crumbs
Salt and pepper to taste
Olive oil for frying

Combine all ingredients except olive oil and mix very well, using your hands to distribute herbs and spices evenly. Shape into small meatballs, about 1 inch in diameter, and fry in olive oil until no longer pink in the middle. Drain on paper towels. Serve with Fresh Cilantro Relish, if desired.

Prep time: 30 minutes
Cooking time: 30 minutes
Yield: about 3 dozen

Fresh Cilantro Relish

Cilantro has been grown in Greece since antiquity. Early cultivators believed a mixture of cilantro, garlic, and white wine to be an aphrodisiac.

1 cup cilantro, chopped
1/2 cup chopped walnuts
2 cloves garlic, minced
1 small green chili, seeded and chopped
1/3 cup lemon juice
Salt to taste

Place all ingredients except lemon juice and salt in the bowl of a food processor and process into a coarse paste. With processor on, gradually add lemon juice. Add salt to taste.

The relish will be very dry. If it's too dry for your palate, stir in a little water.

Prep time: 15 minutes
Yield: 1 cup

Pita Chips

6 pita breads   *Assorted mixed dried herbs such as*
Melted butter   *rosemary, thyme, dill, and oregano*
1 teaspoon garlic powder *Salt and pepper to taste*

Preheat oven to 325°F.

Cut each pita into 12 sections. Arrange the pieces in a single layer on a baking sheet. Brush with melted butter. Sprinkle the garlic powder and mixed herbs over the tops and bake for 8 minutes, or until crisp. Store in an airtight container.

Prep time: 20 minutes
Yield: 72 chips

Sicilian. *Small, green, oval, brine-cured olives. Often bottled with oregano.*

Nicoise. *Tiny black olive from France. Cured in brine and packed in oil, often with Provencal herbs.*

Picholine. *Mild, green, delicate French olives.*

Manzanilla. *Green Spanish olives. The olive most widely consumed in the United States.*

"Greeks never drink without eating and rarely drink without company."
—**Diane Kochilas,** The Food and Wine of Greece

If you have a few grapevines (or a friendly neighbor with a few grapevines), treat yourself to fresh grape leaves for stuffing. Pick young, tender leaves from the ends of the vines. Cut off the stems and wash the leaves thoroughly under running water. Blanch them in boiling salted water for 3 minutes, then plunge them into cold water to stop the cooking. Drain in a colander.

To store grape leaves, stack them in a layer, shiny side down, about 20 deep. Place each stack on a sheet of plastic wrap and roll the entire stack, plastic and all, into a cylinder, squeezing out excess water as you roll. Place the rolls in a plastic bag and freeze for up to six months. When ready to use, place the rolls in warm water until they're thawed and can be separated easily without tearing.

Stuffed Grape Leaves

Although these famous rolls are not difficult to prepare, they are somewhat time-consuming. They freeze well, so they don't have to be prepared very often.

Filling:
1 medium red onion, chopped
1/2 cup chopped scallions
6 tablespoons olive oil
1 cup rice
2 garlic cloves, minced
1 teaspoon ground cumin
Salt and freshly ground pepper to taste
2 cups water
1/4 cup chopped fresh fennel
1/2 cup finely chopped fresh dill
1/2 cup finely chopped parsley
1/4 cup chopped fresh mint (or 1-1/2 teaspoons dried)

Leaves:
1 16-ounce jar grape leaves, or 1/2 pound fresh
2 lemons, thinly sliced
2 cups water
1/4 cup olive oil
Lemon wedges to garnish

Cooking and assembly:

In a skillet, fry the onions and scallions in the olive oil until soft and transparent. Add rice and cook, stirring constantly, for 5 minutes, until grains are lightly browned. Add garlic, cumin, salt, pepper, and water; cover and simmer until rice is softened but not completely cooked and water is absorbed (about 8 minutes). Remove from heat and allow to cool. When rice is cool, stir in fennel, dill, parsley, and mint.

Drain and rinse the grape leaves. Whether you're using fresh or canned leaves, bring enough water to cover leaves to a rolling boil and blanch the leaves for 1 to 2 minutes to soften. Drain leaves in a colander and allow to cool.

Place a leaf, shiny side down, on your work surface and place a heaping tablespoon of filling toward the stem end. Fold up the bottom of the leaf, then fold in the sides, and finish rolling into a neat package. Repeat until you run out of either filling or leaves.

Line the bottom of a heavy pan with vine leaves. Pack the rolls, seam side down, in closely packed rows until the bottom of the pan is covered. Place five or six lemon slices on top and add additional layers until all are in the pan, covering each layer with lemon slices.

Cover the rolls with any remaining grape leaves. Stir together the water and olive oil and pour over the rolls. Invert a heavy plate on top to hold the rolls in place during cooking.

Simmer gently for about 1 hour, checking occasionally to see that they haven't boiled dry. Remove the pan from the heat and set it aside until cool. Carefully remove the rolls from the heat, discarding lemon slices.

Serve at room temperature or chilled, garnishing the platter with lemon wedges.

Yield: about 5 dozen
Prep time: 1-1/2 hours
Cooking time: 1 hour

Canned

If you don't have access to grapevines, jars of leaves packed in brine are available in most large supermarkets. Greece and California are the major producers.

Each jar contains 40 to 50 leaves rolled tightly together. Without dumping the brine—you'll need it later if you have leftovers—carefully remove the leaves all at the same time, to prevent them from tearing. Unroll them, peel off as many as you need, and soak them for 10 or 15 minutes, to reduce the salty, briny taste. Rinse under running water. Return the remaining leaves to the jar of brine and store in the refrigerator, where they will keep for several months.

This delicate pastry can intimidate cooks who are a lot tougher than it is. In reality, packages of frozen phyllo are available at most supermarkets and can be tamed with little trouble.

Thaw the entire package in the refrigerator. When you're ready to work, gently unfold the dough. You will have a stack of very thin sheets of phyllo. Peel a single sheet off the stack, place it on your work surface, and proceed with the directions in the recipe. As you work, keep the unused portion of the dough covered with a clean, damp cloth. If phyllo dries out—which it will do instanta-neously, especially around the edges, if left uncovered—it will become brittle.

Wrap leftover phyllo in plastic wrap, roll it up, and place in the refrigerator, where it will keep for a few days before drying out.

Spinach and Feta Phyllo Triangles

If stuffed grape leaves are the most famous Greek dish, this is surely second. Incredibly crisp and tender, phyllo dough is delectable and easy to work with.

10-ounce package frozen chopped spinach, thawed and squeezed dry
  (or 1 cup blanched, chopped fresh spinach)
1 pound feta cheese, crumbled
3 tablespoons lemon juice, freshly squeezed
2 tablespoons grated onion
1 clove garlic, crushed
2 teaspoons fresh dill
1 teaspoon fresh oregano
1/4 teaspoon freshly ground pepper
2 eggs
1/2 cup chopped parsley
1 pound frozen phyllo pastry sheets, thawed
1/2 cup butter, melted

Preheat oven to 350°F.

In a large bowl, combine all ingredients except phyllo and butter, and mix well.

Unroll the phyllo dough on a work surface. Keep covered with a moist cloth until ready for use. (See "Working with Phyllo.")

Place two phyllo sheets on the work surface, one on top of the other, and dab lightly with butter, especially the edges. Top with two more sheets and dab with butter again.

Cut the buttered phyllo lengthwise into 6 strips. (Each strip will have four layers of dough.) Place 1 tablespoon of the spinach mixture on a phyllo strip, close to the end near-est you. Roll up the strip of phyllo flag style (see the illustration), making sure to seal the edges by brushing with melted butter. Place the folded triangle on the baking sheet.

Fill and fold the remaining strips of phyllo in a similar fashion.

Repeat the buttering, filling, and folding until you run out of sheets of phyllo or filling.

Brush tops of pastries with butter and bake 20 minutes, or until golden.

Prep time: 1 hour
Yield: about 48 pastries

Taramasalata

Essentially a sea-flavored mayonnaise, this everyday Greek dip contains carp roe *(tarama)*, which is available in most Greek and many Middle Eastern markets.

2 slices white bread, crusts removed
1/3 cup tarama
1 tablespoon grated onion
1/4 cup freshly squeezed lemon juice
3/4 cup olive oil
Finely chopped parsley to garnish

Tear the bread into pieces and soak it in water until it's saturated. Squeeze it dry.

Place the bread, tarama, onion, and lemon juice in a blender. Add 1/4 cup of the olive oil and blend until smooth. With the blender running, slowly add the remaining oil, maintaining a thin, steady stream. It should emulsify into a creamy sauce. If it is too thick, add up to 1/4 cup more olive oil. Chill, sprinkle with chopped parsley, and serve with pita chips (see recipe on page 27), crackers, celery, cucumber sticks, or black olives on toothpicks.

Prep time: 20 minutes
Yield: About 1-1/2 cups

MARATHON

Marathon *is the Greek word
for "fennel," an exquisite,
licorice-flavored herb common in Greek cooking. The
famous Battle of Marathon
in 490 B.C.—in which the
Greeks defeated the Persians
and sent the news home to
Athens by way of a long-
distance runner—was so
named because the battlefield
was covered with fennel.*

Tabouleh

This Middle Eastern staple is becoming increasingly popular worldwide. It tastes fresh and uncluttered.

*3/4 cup bulgar wheat
2 cups cold water
2 cups chopped parsley
3/4 cup scallions, finely chopped
1/2 cup fresh mint, finely chopped
1/2 cup lemon juice, freshly squeezed
1/2 cup virgin olive oil
Salt and freshly ground pepper to taste
3 ripe tomatoes, peeled, seeded, and diced
1 medium cucumber, seeded and diced*

Soak the bulgar in the water for 30 minutes. Drain it through a fine sieve, extracting as much moisture as possible, and spread it onto a cloth to dry further. It is essential that the bulgar be as dry as possible.

Place chopped parsley in a towel, wrap it up, run under cool water to rinse, and wring it dry. Repeat until rinse water runs clear.

Place the bulgar, parsley, scallions, and mint in a large bowl. Stir to mix well.

In another bowl, beat together the lemon juice and olive oil. Season with salt and pepper. Add this sauce to the bulgar and toss the two together. Add just enough sauce to make the salad moist but not runny.

Gently fold in the tomatoes and cucumbers. Cover and chill. To serve, place the tabouleh in crisp romaine hearts or serve with pita chips.

Prep time: 30 minutes
Yield: 8 to 10 servings

Baba Ghanoush

An eggplant and sesame puree, this Middle Eastern specialty is luxurious in texture and taste.

1 medium eggplant
1/4 cup lemon juice, freshly squeezed
1/4 cup tahini
2 cloves garlic, minced
Salt and freshly ground pepper to taste
1 tablespoon fruity olive oil
1/4 cup finely chopped parsley

Preheat the oven to 375°F.

Place the whole eggplant on a lightly oiled baking sheet and roast it, turning occasionally, until quite soft, about 30 to 45 minutes. Remove from oven and cool slightly. While still warm, peel off the skin and remove stem end.

Place the eggplant, lemon juice, tahini, and garlic in a food processor and process until smooth. Season with salt and pepper.

Transfer the puree to a mixing bowl and beat in the olive oil and parsley. Refrigerate for several hours before serving. Bring to room temperature to serve. Serve with raw vegetables or pita chips.

Prep time: 10 minutes
Cooking time: 45 minutes
Yield: 1-1/2 cups

EGGPLANT

"The poor man's caviar," it's often called—high praise indeed for a vegetable. Eggplants are glossy-skinned and gorgeous. They range from small, round, and white (hence the name) to huge, voluptuous ovals of mauve, violet, blue-black, and the deepest purple. Thais even grow small, green eggplants the size of peas.

A native of India, eggplants were brought by Arab traders to Spain and North Africa during the Middle Ages. Three centuries later, eggplants had established themselves all over the Mediterranean.

Eggplants are water-filled vegetables, and the moisture is often bitter. To extract it, slice the eggplant and salt the slices well. Place them in a colander and allow them to drain at least 30 minutes. Rinse and pat dry.

An eggplant's spongy flesh soaks up oil by the cupful. To avoid a greasy product, sauté in a nonstick pan, using as little oil as possible. When purchasing eggplant, check for tender skin. If the skin feels tough, it will need to be peeled before cooking.

TAHINI

Used in a variety of Middle Eastern dishes, tahini ("tah-HEE-nee") is a paste of ground sesame seeds. Like peanut butter, it is rich in protein, oil, and taste. It is available, canned, in many supermarkets and most specialty food stores.

34

H u m m u s

With its wonderful combination of flavors, this Middle Eastern dip is terrific with pita toasts or raw vegetables—carrots, cauliflower, celery, and bell peppers of any hue.

3 cups canned chick-peas, rinsed and drained
1/3 cup tahini
1/2 cup lemon juice
2 cloves garlic, crushed
2 teaspoons ground cumin
1 teaspoon ground coriander
1/8 teaspoon cayenne
Salt and freshly ground pepper to taste
Fresh parley and lemon slices (for garnish)

Although it is time-consuming (and optional), removing the skins from the chick-peas will improve the texture of the finished dip, making it almost silky.

Place all the ingredients in a food processor and process to a smooth paste.

Transfer the puree to a serving dish. Garnish with the parsley and lemon slices. Serve with raw vegetables or pita chips.

Prep time: 10 minutes
Yield: 3 cups

Stuffed Mussels

Often called "the poor man's oyster," mussels give poverty a good name. These delicious mollusks are quite easy to prepare.

30 mussels
1 cup water
1/2 cup white wine
2 large onions, finely chopped
1/4 cup olive oil
1/2 cup short-grain rice, rinsed

1/3 cup pine nuts
1/4 cup currants, soaked in water
   15 minutes and drained
1/4 teaspoon ground allspice
2 teaspoons chopped fresh dill
Salt and freshly ground pepper to taste

To prepare the mussels:

Mussels should be unbroken and tightly closed. Discard any that are wide open or have broken shells. If mussel is slightly open, tap the shell smartly with a hard object. If the mussel closes up, it may be used; if not, discard it.

Place the mussels in a colander under running water and scrub them with a stiff brush to remove any debris. Use scissors to clip off the stringy beards.

Combine the mussels, water, and wine in a large saucepan. Cover and cook over medium high heat for 5 minutes, or until they open. Discard any mussels that do not open.

To prepare the filling:

Saute the onions in the oil until soft and translucent. Add remaining filling ingredients and simmer slowly for about 15 minutes, or until liquid is absorbed.

Assembly and cooking:

Place 2 teaspoons of filling in each mussel and close the shell as much as possible. Place the shells in a Dutch oven or large pan and add water to be 1 inch deep. Invert a heavy plate on top to keep mussels closed. Bring to a boil, cover, and simmer for 30 minutes. Turn off heat and leave mussels in pan to cool.

Prep time: 1 hour
Yield: 8 servings

WHITE HATS, BLACK HATS

During the Turkish occupation of Greece (which lasted from 1453 until 1821), many Greek chefs were given refuge in monasteries. To differentiate themselves from the monks, who wore the tall, cylindrical, black hats common to the Greek Orthodox church, the chefs donned tall, white hats, which ultimately became the standard chef's hat that is now universal.

China

Defining Ingredients

Spice mixtures, soy sauce, tofu, cloves, star anise, rice wine and vinegar, oriental vegetables (bamboo shoots, water chestnuts, bean sprouts, as well as cucumbers, radishes, and scallions), Szechuan peppers, hoisin sauce, egg roll and wonton wrappers

Chinese cooks assert that their cuisine includes 80,000 dishes, and it's a claim easy to believe. The oldest continuous civilization in the world, China has had a long time to develop a tradition of cooking and eating. A thousand years before the birth of Christ, Chinese cooks were creating elaborate dishes and keeping track of their recipes on squares of silk.

Confucius proclaimed that the enjoyment of good food was one of the gentle pastimes that brought peace and harmony to a society. Artists, writers, and intellectuals were expected to be gourmets, and cooking and eating were raised to art forms.

Of all Asian cuisines, China's is probably the most widely known outside Asia. Cantonese food is the most familiar of China's regional styles. Named for the southeastern port city

DISTINCTIVE CHINESE SEASONINGS

■

Five-Spice Powder

A famous Chinese spice combination, this finely ground, ready-mixed powder consists of star anise, aniseed, cloves, cinnamon, and fennel. It is used to flavor marinades and as a dipping salt. Fragrant, slightly sweet, and very pungent, it is best used sparingly.

Szechuan Peppercorns

Unrelated to black peppercorns, these small, hard, pepperlike seeds have a strong and pungent aroma. They are often sold whole and in bulk, thorns and all. As with other herbs and spices, store in an airtight container.

Dried Shrimp

These tiny, very strong-tasting shrimp can overwhelm a Western palate in the amounts common in Chinese cooking. They are powerful seasonings, but

of Canton, Cantonese cooking relies on a few seasonings—soy sauce, ginger, wine—and specializes in stir-frying, roasting, and steaming. The wonderful tradition of dim sum—feasting on a great many small servings of different foods—originated here. Since the Cantonese have always been adventurous travelers, the first Chinese restaurants in other countries cooked Cantonese, which came to be identified with all of Chinese food.

With the recent trend in hot and spicy food, Szechwan cooking has become increasingly popular. Peppery, spicy, somewhat oily, loaded with chili peppers, garlic, and ginger, Szechwan cooking is among the hottest in China. Also spicy is the cooking from the province of Honan, with its strongly flavored, sweet-and-sour dishes.

The cooking of Peking tends toward light, elegant dishes seasoned with leeks, garlic, and scallions. Peking gave us the famous duck, as well as delectable spring rolls.

On the east coast, Fukien province is renowned for its soy sauce (said to be the best in the country), its seafood, and its soups. At least two soups are served at most family meals. At banquets, as many as one-quarter of all courses may be clear soups.

With its emphasis on lightly cooked fresh vegetables, Chinese cooking has influenced much of the world's thinking about food for generations.

Fried Wontons

This irresistible snack can be eaten alone or dipped in Shanghai Sauce.

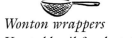

Wonton wrappers
Vegetable oil for deep frying

Leaving the wonton wrappers in the neat stack in which they were packaged, cut the wrappers into strips about 1/2 inch wide, cutting through as many layers as you can. Separate the cut piles into individual strips.

In a deep-fryer or wok, heat oil to medium hot (350°F). Deep-fry the wontons a handful at a time until crisp. This will take only a few seconds, so don't wander off. Remove from oil with slotted spoon or wire-mesh scoop and drain on several layers of paper towels.

Prep time: 5 minutes
Cooking time: 10 minutes

Barbecued Ribs

2 cups rice vinegar
2/3 cup soy sauce
1 cup honey
4 tablespoons finely chopped shallots
2 cloves garlic, minced

1 teaspoon finely chopped fresh ginger
1/4 cup dry sherry
1/4 cup white wine
1/4 cup vermouth
4 pounds pork spareribs, parboiled for 3 minutes

Combine all ingredients except ribs in a bowl and whisk until smooth. Pour the marinade over the ribs, toss to coat, and refrigerate overnight.

Preheat oven to 325°F. Place the ribs on a rack that's set in a roasting pan and bake, uncovered, for 1 hour. Baste ribs occasionally with the drippings. Serve with Shanghai Sauce.

Prep time: 1-1/2 hours + overnight marinating
Yield: 8 servings

Shanghai Sauce

Serve with Barbecued Ribs or as a dipping sauce for Fried Wontons.

1-1/2 cups hoisin sauce
1 cup canned, drained, crushed tomatoes
1-1/2 tablespoons sriracha sauce
  (or Tabasco)
1 cup chicken stock

3 tablespoons fresh orange juice
2 tablespoons sesame oil
2 tablespoons oyster sauce
1/2 tablespoon garlic powder
1/2 teaspoon ground ginger

Whisk all ingredients together.

Prep time: 10 minutes
Yield: about 4 cups

they're often that indefinable "something" that's missing from a Chinese dish prepared by Westerners. Dried shrimp are available in oriental markets.

Soy Sauce

Derived from fermented soybeans, wheat, yeast, and salt, soy sauce is a mainstay in the Chinese kitchen. It is available in two grades, light and dark. The light variety is preferred for everyday use as a table condiment, while the dark is used for barbecuing and for thick sauces.

39

Hoisin Sauce

This spicy sauce is also made from fermented soybeans, but with the addition of sugar, garlic, and chili. Sweet and reddish brown, it is used primarily for marinades and dipping sauces. It will keep indefinitely when refrigerated.

Bean Sauces and Pastes

Westerners are happy to cook with these sauces and pastes but usually consider them too strong and pungent for use as condiments. Bean sauces and pastes are quite common, however, on the Chinese table. They are made from a variety of beans (usually described by color) and range from "sweet" to pungent. They are sometimes irreplaceable as ingredients in Chinese dishes.

Strange Flavor Eggplant

Eggplants are prominent in Chinese food. This strange and wonderful dip is excellent with fried wontons.

2 medium eggplants
2 tablespoons minced garlic
2 tablespoons minced pickled ginger
  (available at oriental markets)
1/2 cup chopped scallions
1 teaspoon red pepper flakes, crushed
1/3 cup soy sauce
1/3 cup brown sugar
1 tablespoon rice vinegar
2 tablespoons hot water
1/3 cup plus 2 tablespoons sesame oil

Preheat oven to 475°F.

Prick the skin of the eggplants in several places. Place them on a baking sheet and roast for approximately 30 minutes, or until tender.

After the eggplants have cooled somewhat but are still warm, cut them open and scrape the pulp into the bowl of a food processor. Puree until smooth.

In a small bowl, combine the garlic, ginger, scallions, and red pepper flakes. In another bowl combine the soy sauce, brown sugar, rice vinegar, and hot water.

Place 2 tablespoons of the sesame oil in a frying pan or wok and swirl to coat. Heat to moderately high. Add the dry seasoning mixture and stir-fry very briefly until fragrant. Add the liquid mixture and bring to a boil.

Add the eggplant puree and bring to a boil again. Remove from the heat and stir in the 1/3 cup sesame oil. Adjust the seasonings to taste.

Refrigerate the puree overnight, to allow the flavors to blend.

Serve at room temperature.

Prep time: 1 hour
Yield: about 2 cups

Egg Rolls

2 tablespoons vegetable oil
1 teaspoon minced garlic
1 teaspoon minced fresh ginger
1 tablespoon peanut butter
2 cups fine julienned carrots
5 cups julienned cabbage
1 cup julienned red pepper
3/4 cup scallions, sliced on the bias
2 cups cooked rice noodles, cut into 2" lengths
2 tablespoons light soy sauce
Lumpia or egg roll wrappers
Vegetable oil for deep frying

Heat the 2 tablespoons vegetable oil in a large frying pan. Add garlic and ginger, stir-frying quickly to avoid burning. Add the peanut butter and stir to dissolve. Add all vegetables and stir-fry for 2 minutes. Add rice noodles and soy sauce, and cook for 2 or 3 more minutes. Transfer all ingredients to a colander and drain. Refrigerate overnight.

With a corner of a lumpia wrapper facing you, place 3 heaping tablespoons of mixture along the center. Fold up the bottom corner of the wrapper over the filling and roll once. Fold in the sides and continue to roll into a cylinder, moistening the edges with water to seal.

Heat the vegetable oil in a skillet or deep fryer to medium-hot (375°F). Deep-fry the rolls 5 or 6 at a time, turning, until golden brown.

Prep time: 45 minutes
Yield: 24 rolls

FINDING EXOTIC INGREDIENTS

■

Don't be put off by a recipe that calls for ingredients you've never heard of. If you like to shop at all, tracking them down is half the fun. (Hint: The worse the English translation on the label, the higher the quality of the food inside.)

Where to start?

■ *Many large supermarkets carry an array of fresh and canned ingredients, especially Mexican, Chinese, and Thai.*

■ *"Natural" food stores are excellent sources of Middle Eastern ingredients and whole bulk spices.*

■ *Ethnic groceries—oriental, Latin American, or Indian—are obvious sources with wide selections.*

■ *Part of the joy of exploring a new city is visiting specialty shops of interest: sprawling on the hotel bed with the phone directory, searching for*

Chinese Chicken Wings

24 chicken wings (4 to 5 pounds) 1 tablespoon ground ginger
1 cup soy sauce 1 tablespoon garlic powder
6 tablespoons sesame oil 1 tablespoon dry mustard
4 tablespoons sriracha (or Tabasco) 1 tablespoon onion powder

Place the chicken wings in a large bowl. Whisk the remaining ingredients together and pour over the wings, turning to coat. Cover and refrigerate overnight, turning occasionally.

Preheat the oven to 375°F. With wing tips down, place chicken wings on rack in roasting pan and bake 20 minutes. Turn, baste with the marinade, and bake another 20 minutes.

Alternatively, place wings on a preheated grill over medium-hot coals and cook 20 minutes or until done, turning and basting occasionally.

Prep time: 10 minutes
Resting time: overnight
Cooking time: 20 to 40 minutes
Yield: 8 servings

Shrimp Toast

12 slices white bread, crusts removed 4 teaspoons fresh ginger, minced
1 pound fresh, small or medium shrimp, 1-1/2 teaspoons salt
   peeled and deveined 4 egg whites, beaten
4 tablespoons scallions, chopped 4 tablespoons cornstarch
4 tablespoons water chestnuts, chopped Black and white sesame seeds
2 ounces pork fat, chopped Peanut oil for frying

Cut the slices of bread into quarters. Allow them to dry out completely (about an hour or two).

In a food processor, blend the remaining ingredients, except for the sesame seeds, until a smooth paste is formed. Spread the paste over the bread slices and sprinkle alternately with the two kinds of sesame seeds.

Heat oil to medium hot (350°F). Fry the shrimp toasts slowly until crisp and golden, about 3 to 4 minutes. Remove toasts from oil with slotted spoon and drain on paper towels.

Prep time: 30 minutes
Yield: 48 pieces

Cucumber Fans

These marinated cucumbers have a light, refreshing taste.

1 pound slim, firm cucumbers	*1 tablespoon vegetable oil*
(2 to 3 medium)	*3 to 5 drops oriental sesame oil*
2 teaspoons coarse salt	*1-1/2 teaspoons finely chopped fresh ginger*
2 teaspoons soy sauce	*1 tablespoon minced garlic*
2 tablespoons rice vinegar	*1/2 teaspoon Szechuan peppercorns*
3 tablespoons sugar	*1/2 teaspoon dried red chili flakes*

Trim off the ends and cut the cucumbers into pieces 1 inch long. Cut the pieces in half lengthwise.

To make a fan, place a cucumber piece cut-side-down and make comblike incisions along one edge, spacing the cuts about 1/8 inch apart and cutting almost to the other side. Be careful to stop the cuts about 1/8 inch from the opposite side, so that all the cucumber remains in one piece. Pull the thin slices apart for a fan shape.

Sprinkle the fans with the salt and set aside for 20 or 30 minutes. When a puddle of water collects in the bottom of the bowl, drain and rinse the fans and squeeze them gently to remove excess water.

Stir together the soy sauce, rice vinegar, and sugar until the sugar is partially dissolved.

In a wok or medium skillet, heat both oils over medium heat. Add ginger, garlic, peppercorns, and chili flakes, and sauté for about 10 seconds. Add the cucumbers and

mystery bookstores or bead shops or fabric houses. If you cook internationally, you'll find yourself thumbing through a whole new category: "Groceries, Indian," or "Supermarkets, Thai."

■ *Be bold. Salespeople in exotic groceries are used to dealing with customers who are, from their point of view, breathtakingly ignorant and possibly deranged. When you enter an Asian market in search of red curry paste, either you can spend two hours staring at incomprehensible labels, or you can ask—and be led to it in 30 seconds. Either course is satisfying, depending on the amount of time you have.*

■ *In a foreign market, you'll frequently stand in line next to people who look and/or sound as if they belong there, and who are buying the same ingredients you are. They will probably examine your market basket with a friendly mixture of encouragement, amusement, and skepticism. Smile. If they smile back, ask*

43

them what they're going to make with their lemon grass. At best, you'll learn of a new dish. At worst, they will consider you deranged.

■ The second or third time you shop in a foreign market, the merchant will get chatty, asking after your successes and failures. Congratulations! You now have someone to talk to who likes this food as much as you do and who knows a lot more about it. Some of his/her best customers are probably deranged.

44

toss to combine. Add the soy-vinegar-sugar mixture and stir until the mixture is hot, then remove from the heat.

Place the cucumbers in a shallow bowl and pour the sauce over them. Let cool. The dish is at its best if refrigerated overnight and then returned to room temperature.

Prep time: 20 minutes
Yield: 6 servings

Pork Dumplings with Szechuan Dipping Sauce

Traditionally, these are cooked in a bamboo steamer—a marvelous construction of bamboo trays that can be stacked over boiling water in a wok. Any steamer will work, even a rack placed over boiling water in a soup pot.

2 bunches scallions, green parts only
1 pound boneless pork shoulder, finely ground
6 dried Chinese black mushrooms,
    soaked in hot water for 20 minutes
1 cup Chinese cabbage, washed, dried,
    trimmed, and diced
1/2 cup minced leeks
1 tablespoon minced garlic
2 tablespoons minced fresh ginger

2 tablespoons soy sauce
2 tablespoons Chinese rice wine
    or dry sherry
1-1/2 teaspoons sesame oil
1/2 teaspoon sugar
1/4 teaspoon freshly ground pepper
1-1/2 teaspoons cornstarch
48 round dumpling wrappers

First make scallion ties for binding the dumplings. Cut the leaves lengthwise in quarters. Soak in warm water to soften, at least 1 minute. You'll need a total of 48 ties.

Place all remaining ingredients except dumpling wrappers in a large mixing bowl and stir well to combine.

To assemble the dumplings, hold a wrapper in the palm of your hand, cupping it slightly. Place 1 tablespoon filling in the center of the skin. Gather the sides around the filling, squeezing gently. Tie the top of the wrapper with a scallion tie. Repeat with remaining wrappers. Carefully cover the dumplings with plastic wrap until ready to steam.

Prepare the steamer by lining the trays with lightly oiled parchment paper, cornhusks, or banana leaves. Fill a large pot (big enough to hold the steamer) with enough water to come within an inch of the bottom rack. Bring water to a boil. Place the dumplings in the steamer racks and steam, tightly covered, for about 20 minutes or until done, switching racks halfway through.

If the steaming needs to be done in batches, cover the cooked dumplings to keep them warm and reheat in the steamer before serving if necessary.

Prep time: 1 hour
Yield: 48 dumplings

Szechuan Sauce for Dumplings

1/2 cup soy sauce
2 tablespoons finely chopped scallions
1 clove garlic, minced
1-1/2 teaspoons white vinegar

2 teaspoons sesame oil
1/2 teaspoon minced ginger
1 teaspoon sugar
1 to 8 drops hot chili oil or 100% sesame chili oil

Stir all ingredients together.

Prep time: 10 minutes
Yield: about 3/4 cup

SCALLION FLOWERS

A common garnish for oriental meals, scallion flowers are easy to make. Trim the roots and cut off the green leaves about 2 inches above the white part of the scallion. Peel off any wilted outer leaves.

To curl the white end, place a sharp knife against the bottom of the scallion and cut straight up into the scallion about 1 inch. Turn the knife 90 degrees and make a second cut perpendicular to the first. Continue for at least two more cuts, slicing the scallion into finer wedges. Place the scallion in a bowl of ice water for about 10 minutes, or until the "petals" curl.

The green end is curled in a similar fashion. Using a small pair of kitchen shears, cut straight down the length of the green, or stem, end. Continue to cut the leaves into thin strips. Place the scallion in a bowl of ice water for about 10 minutes, or until it curls enough to suit you.

Morocco

Defining Ingredients

Lemons, olives, dates, almonds, flower water, mint, cinnamon, saffron, cumin, turmeric, ginger, cilantro, cayenne

All Moroccan food is finger food. With the help of a spongy, delicious bread—an excellent implement as well as a staple food—and seated on cushions around a low table, Moroccans enjoy a cuisine that is rapidly gaining international currency.

Three great dishes are central to Moroccan food. Best known is *couscous,* the name for both the fine, fluffy, rice-size grain of semolina wheat and the dish of which it forms the center. Couscous is cooked in a porous steamer over a bubbling, spiced stew; steam from the stew both cooks and seasons the grain, which is served with the stew and its flavorful gravy.

Another famous dish is the *tagine*—a slowly simmered stew of lamb, chicken, or vegetables. The most famous version consists of chicken, olives, and preserved lemons seasoned with saffron, ginger, and cumin.

A third great dish is *bisteeya*—layers of spiced chicken, eggs, and almonds in a flaky, paper-thin crust (see the recipe on page 52).

While not perhaps the most significant culinary contribution, the Moroccan passion for mint tea may be the most indelible. Anyone who has savored an after-dinner cup of hot mint tea lightly sweetened with honey for a few nights

BELL PEPPERS

Although peppers are a defining ingredient in a number of cuisines—Thai, Indian, Italian—they are native to the New World. From Hungarian paprika to the sweet green peppers popular in Morocco, peppers are Central American by birth.

Devoid of the capsaicin that gives chili peppers their heat, bell peppers contribute a sweet, mellow flavor and gorgeous colors: red, yellow, orange, even purple. Bell peppers are adept at changing colors. Green peppers are exactly that—green, or unripe—and, left on the vine, will mature into other, brighter hues. Rich purple peppers, alas, revert to green when cooked.

running is probably hooked for life. (Of all its herbal properties, mint is best known worldwide as a digestif.)

Moroccan cities are famous for their *souks*—open-air markets where a careful shopper can buy anything from camels to cilantro. Stalls are piled high with fresh oranges and fresh and preserved lemons (a Moroccan hallmark), fresh and ground herbs and spices, carrots, tomatoes, and peppers. Live chickens squawk their protests, and customers and vendors debate the proper definition of a "reasonable price."

The native people of Morocco are Berbers. In 683 the country was invaded by Arabs, as part of the same expansionist movement that led to the Muslim conquest of Spain in 711. Separated from each other only by the narrow Strait of Gibraltar, Muslim Morocco and Muslim Spain maintained close cultural contact for centuries, a relationship clear even today in the foods of both countries. Morocco has also been influenced enormously by the Middle Eastern food brought to the country centuries ago.

A reliance on stews of tender meats and vegetables, a love of subtly flavored grains, a fluency with spices and herbs—all these make Moroccan food a delightful discovery.

Tomato and Green Pepper Salad

This is one of the most common dishes in Morocco.

3 green peppers, roasted, peeled, cored, and seeded
4 large tomatoes, skinned and seeded
2 tablespoons olive oil
1 tablespoon lemon juice, freshly squeezed
1 clove garlic, peeled and crushed

1/2 teaspoon ground cumin
Pinch sweet paprika
1/2 teaspoon salt
1/4 teaspoon freshly ground pepper
1/4 preserved lemon

Cut the peppers and tomatoes into bite-size pieces and place them in a mixing bowl. Add all remaining ingredients except the preserved lemon and gently toss to blend.

Peel the lemon skin away from the pulp and finely chop the peel. Sprinkle over the vegetables.

Prep time: 15 minutes
Yield: 4 servings

Preserved Lemons

A hallmark of Moroccan cooking, preserved lemons are worth incorporating into your cooking even if you never make another Moroccan dish. Wonderfully tart and exotic-tasting, they have a myriad of uses.

1/2 cup salt   *1 cinnamon stick (optional)*
6 lemons   *Additional freshly squeezed lemon juice (if necessary)*

Sprinkle enough salt into a mason jar or plastic container with tight-fitting lid to cover the bottom. Quarter the lemons lengthwise, stopping the cuts just short of the stem end. The lemon wedges should remain attached at one end. Spread the lemons open and sprinkle salt on the pulp. Reclose the lemons.

Pack the lemons into the jar, pressing them down and adding additional salt between layers. Add the cinnamon stick, if desired. If the pressed lemons don't release enough juice to cover, add additional freshly squeezed lemon juice until all lemons are completely covered.

Cover the jar and allow the lemons to ripen for 30 days, shaking the jar occasionally. There is no need to refrigerate.

When ready for use, rinse the lemons thoroughly to remove the salt. Most people use just the peel, but the pulp can also be added to dishes for extra flavor. Reserve the lemon juice for the next jar of lemons.

Prep time: 20 minutes
Yield: peel of 6 lemons

Almond-Stuffed Dates

Moroccans make excellent use of almond paste, stuffing everything from whole cooked fish to simple dates.

16 dates   *16 whole almonds*   *6 tablespoons almond paste*

Slice each date lengthwise down one side and pull the edges open. Stuff each date with 1 almond and 1 teaspoon almond paste.

Prep time: 15 minutes
Yield: 16 dates

DATES

■

It is a Moroccan tradition to welcome guests with dates and milk, as signs of hospitality and abundance. The fruit of a palm tree native to India, dates were exported to the Mediterranean region and to Western Europe before the Christian era. Now they're grown practically everywhere there are desert conditions.

Fruit is our sweetest natural food, and dates are the sweetest of the sweet. About 60% of their dry weight is sugar, compared to 10% to 15% for most temperate-zone fruit and a sour 1% for lemons and limes.

49

Little known in the West, flower waters are routinely used by Moroccan cooks. Rosewater is the diluted essence extracted from dark red roses grown especially for this purpose. Orange flower water is derived from the bergamot (sour orange) tree, widely grown in Spain, just across the Strait of Gibraltar. Flower waters are added directly to the food in small quantities, and the results can be exquisite.

FAVA BEANS

■

Aptly named, the broad bean (fava or faba *bean) is huge and fleshy. Indigenous to*

Orange and Walnut Salad

Morocco's orange groves produce magnificent fruit, which Moroccans take full advantage of. While not a Moroccan specialty, peppery arugula is a marvelous complement to the orange flavors. Romaine is also good.

2 bunches flavorful lettuce
2 tablespoons lemon juice
2 tablespoons orange juice
2 tablespoons sugar
1 tablespoon orange flower water

1/2 teaspoon cinnamon
Pinch of salt
3 navel oranges
1 cup chopped walnuts

Wash the lettuce and pat dry. To keep it crisp, refrigerate it until you're ready to use it.

In a small bowl, combine the lemon juice, orange juice, sugar, orange flower water, cinnamon, and salt.

Peel the oranges and remove all white membrane. Carefully section the oranges and place in a bowl. Pour any additional juice from the oranges into the dressing.

When ready to serve, gently toss the lettuce with the dressing and place on a serving platter. Arrange the orange segments on top and sprinkle with the chopped walnuts. Sprinkle with additional cinnamon if desired.

Prep time: 15 minutes
Yield: 6 servings

Moroccan Carrots

This traditional salad frequently appears early in the dinner.

1/2 cup mild olive oil
1/8 cup balsamic vinegar
1/2 cup red wine vinegar
3 cloves garlic, coarsely chopped
1/8 cup sweet paprika
1/8 cup ground cumin

Salt to taste
1-1/2 pounds carrots, peeled, trimmed, and cut into diagonal slices about 1/3 inch thick
1/2 cup minced fresh parsley

In a large bowl, whisk together the oil and vinegars. With a mortar and pestle, grind the garlic with the paprika, cumin, and salt. Gradually work in the oil-and-vinegar mixture. If the dressing is too grainy, stir in 1 tablespoon of cold water to smooth.

In a large pot of boiling salted water, cook the carrots on high heat until just tender, about 2 minutes. Drain quickly; do not rinse. Add the hot carrots to the dressing and toss to coat evenly. Stir in the parsley.

Serve at room temperature.

Prep time: 30 minutes
Yield: 6 servings

Fava Bean Dip

Bean dips seem to appear in every culture that has access to legumes.

1 teaspoon cumin seed
1 can cooked fava beans, drained, rinsed, skins removed
3 garlic cloves, peeled
2 to 4 tablespoons extra-virgin olive oil
Salt to taste
1/4 teaspoon dried oregano
Pinch cayenne

Toast the cumin seed in a 350°F oven for 5 minutes.

In a food processor fitted with a metal blade, puree the beans with the garlic and cumin seed. With the motor running, slowly pour in enough olive oil to achieve a soupy consistency. Season with salt.

Transfer to a serving bowl and sprinkle with salt, cumin, oregano, and cayenne. Serve with pita bread.

Prep time: 15 minutes
Yield: 4 servings

Asia and the Mediterranean, crops of favas were cultivated by ancient Egyptians, Greeks, and Romans, despite Pythagoras, who took time off from his famous theorem to hypothesize that fava beans contained the souls of the dead and, as a matter of common courtesy, should not be eaten.

Until the Spanish conquistadors brought Mexican beans back to Spain, favas were the only beans Europeans knew. Today, favas are still regular fare around the Mediterranean and in India and the Middle East.

In a kind of trans-Atlantic bean exchange, the conquistadors carried favas with them to the New World. Barely recognized in North America, fava beans are popular in Mexico and Brazil.

Mint is one of the toughest herbs in any country; it has taken over many a garden and more than one back-yard. Fortunately, it's welcome just about everywhere. It scents everything from candy to toothpaste and is virtually a synonym for "fresh." For centuries it has been used as a breath fresh-ener and is a well-regarded aid to digestion—hence after-dinner mints.

It makes a fine tea, and an after-dinner cup of steam-ing mint tea laced with honey is a Moroccan custom well worth adopting.

Bisteeya

There's no way around it: This is a time-consuming recipe. It's also the Moroccan dish that many a traveler still remembers years later—a truly marvelous creation that belongs on any cook's list of weekend projects. Traditionally made with squab, it's delicious with chicken.

The chicken layer:
1 whole frying chicken,
    about 4-1/2 to 5 pounds
1 onion, finely chopped
3/4 cup chopped parsley
1/4 cup chopped cilantro
Pinch of saffron
1/4 teaspoon turmeric
1 teaspoon freshly ground black pepper
1 teaspoon ground ginger
2 cinnamon sticks, about 6 inches long
Salt to taste
1/2 cup melted butter
4 cups water

The almond layer:
1-1/2 cups blanched and sliced almonds, toasted
3 tablespoons sugar
Zest of 2 lemons
2 teaspoons ground cinnamon

The egg layer:
1/4 cup lemon juice
12 eggs

The pastry:
1-pound package phyllo pastry, thawed if frozen
1/2 cup melted butter
Confectioner's sugar for garnish

The day before serving:

Wash the chicken, cleaning the cavities well. Put the chicken in a large soup pot or a large roasting pan with a lid. Add the giblets, onion, herbs and spices, 1/2 cup butter, salt, and water. Bring to a boil, lower the heat, and simmer, covered, for 1 hour.

Meanwhile, in a food processor, coarsely grind the almonds with the sugar, lemon zest, and ground cinnamon. Set aside.

Remove the chicken, giblets, cinnamon sticks, and any loose bones from the pot. Reserve the chicken and giblets. Reduce the liquid in the pot to approximately 2 cups by boiling rapidly, uncovered. Add the lemon juice.

In a large mixing bowl, whisk the eggs until frothy. Pour them into the liquid in the pot and stir until the eggs cook over moderate heat and become curdy and dry. Taste for seasoning, adding salt if necessary. Drain cooked eggs in a colander.

Once the chicken is cool, skin, bone, and shred it. Chop the giblets.

Store the egg mixture, almond mixture, and chicken separately in the refrigerator overnight.

The day of serving:

Preheat the oven to 375°F.

Unroll the phyllo dough and cover with a damp towel. Butter a round, edged baking pan at least 12 inches in diameter. Place one sheet of phyllo in the pan, brush with melted butter, and sprinkle with some of the almond mixture. Place six more sheets of phyllo on the bottom, arranging them around the circumference of the pan so that the bottom is completely covered and the phyllo extends over the edges of the pan. As you add each sheet, brush it with the butter, especially the edges, and sprinkle with some of the almond mixture.

Raise oven temperature to 425°F.

Place the shredded chicken and giblets in an even layer on top of the pastry. Now add the drained egg mixture, again in an even layer. Add a layer of the almond mixture, reserving a portion for the final sheets of pastry.

Cover the layered pie with 8 more sheets of phyllo, repeating the buttering and almond-coating process.

Cover the entire pie with 2 sheets of phyllo (unbuttered and un-almonded), tucking the ends around the edges to seal. Brush the entire pie with the remaining clarified butter, coating the edges heavily.

Bake the pie until the top is golden brown, approximately 20 minutes. Remove from the oven, invert the pie onto a baking sheet, and return to the oven for 10 more minutes, or until golden.

Remove from the oven and invert again onto a serving platter. Dust the top with confectioner's sugar. Serve at once.

Prep and cooking time: 4 to 4-1/2 hours
Yield: 12 to 15 servings.

Italy

Defining Ingredients

*Tomatoes (especially beefsteak and plum types),
basil, oregano, olive oil, olives, garlic, cheese*

A tavola non s'invecchia, says an old Tuscan proverb—
"one doesn't age at the table," which may explain why so
many of us spend so much time there.

Unlike the cuisine of France, famed for its technique, or
the cooking of India, which is dominated by spices, Italian
food centers around a few basic ingredients that Italians
have loved and prepared to perfection for hundreds of years.
Because of their prominence, the quality of those ingredients—the freshness of the vegetables, the purity of the olive
oil, the sharpness of the cheese—is of paramount impor-
tance. Thus, in Italy, as in many other countries where good
food is revered, shopping is still a daily affair whenever time
and circumstance permit.

An Italian market is a feast for the senses: brilliant gold
squash blossoms, ready to be stuffed and fried…huge
bunches of fresh basil…purple heads of garlic…wild mushrooms of every stripe and hue…eggplants in various rich
shades of purple and mauve…bunches of peppery arugula,

ROASTING PEPPERS

Roasted bell peppers—red, yellow, and orange—are delicious snacks that are popular in Italy, Spain, and the United States, as well as important ingredients in various dishes.

Peppers can be roasted over any source of high heat. They must be turned several times during roasting, so that the skin blackens and chars on all sides.

Stove top

Pierce a pepper with a long-handled cooking fork and hold it over a hot burner, either gas or electric. The disadvantage of this method is that you can roast only one pepper at a time, unless you are exceptionally adroit.

Broiler

Set the peppers on a rack and broil, 1 to 2 inches from the heat.

that marvelous salad green that hints of mustard… and stall after stall of fresh, firm, Italian bread.

An Italian kitchen may be the shortest distance between market and table. In their brief passage, vegetables and herbs, fish and fowl are seasoned, combined, and cooked, but they never lose their identity. They remain the glories of the Italian table.

Fritto Misto

For this traditional finger food, use only the freshest of vegetables—carrots, red onions, scallions, mushrooms, green beans, potatoes, and eggplant. Don't omit the lemon wedges; a squirt of fresh lemon juice is essential for this dish.

*5 cups assorted vegetables, cut 1/4 inch
   thick and in a variety of shapes*
2 egg yolks
3 tablespoons olive oil
1 teaspoon salt

1 cup water
1/4 cup white wine, chilled
1-1/2 cups all-purpose flour
Vegetable oil for frying
Lemon wedges

With a whisk, blend the egg yolks and olive oil in a medium bowl. Combine the salt, water, and wine. Whisk into the egg mixture, pouring in a thin, steady stream. Add the flour, a tablespoon at a time, whisking constantly. Allow batter to sit, refrigerated, for 2 hours.

In a deep fryer or large, heavy-bottomed pan, heat the vegetable oil to medium hot (375°F). Dip several of the vegetables into the batter, coating them well. Lower the vegetables into the oil with a slotted spoon or long-handled tongs and fry, turning once, until golden brown. Remove and drain on paper towels.

Serve immediately with lemon wedges.

Prep time: 20 minutes
Rest time: 2 hours
Yield: 12 servings

Romaine-Wrapped Figs, Peppers, and Parmesan

The figs, roasted red peppers, and parmesan slices provide a marvelous combination of sweet, mellow, and salty flavors. As for the size of the romaine wrappers, each diner will have to strike his or her own balance: the smaller ones are tenderer and sweeter, but the larger ones hold more.

2 red bell peppers
3 tablespoons fruity olive oil
1 garlic clove, minced
Salt and freshly ground pepper to taste
16 medium to medium-small romaine leaves, washed and patted dry
15 to 20 black mission figs, stemmed and sliced
1/2 pound Parmigiano-Reggiano, sliced thin

Roast the red peppers (see "Roasting Peppers") and remove the stems, seeds, and veins. Slice the peppers and combine with olive oil, garlic, salt, and pepper, mixing well.

Arrange the romaine leaves on a serving platter; place the figs, peppers, and cheese slices in small bowls. To eat, hold a romaine leaf in one hand and place some peppers, figs, and cheese slices in the center, along the rib. Fold into a long tube, any way you can, and eat.

Prep time: 30 minutes
Yield: 8 servings

Crostini

Never wasteful of good food, the Italians devised this ingenious use for day-old bread.

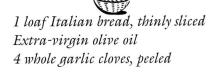

1 loaf Italian bread, thinly sliced
Extra-virgin olive oil
4 whole garlic cloves, peeled

Charcoal grill

Grill the peppers close to very hot coals. Peppers roasted over wood or charcoal will taste decidedly smoky, which can be either delightful or intrusive, depending on your purpose.

Once the peppers are charred on all sides, place them in a plastic or brown paper bag for 10 minutes, to help loosen the skins. (They will continue to cook in the bag; if you want a crunchy pepper, you might skip this step.) Peel off the charred skin, scraping off any stubborn bits with a knife. Slice the peppers open and remove the core and seeds.

To turn roasted peppers into an instant snack, drizzle them with a little olive oil, red wine vinegar, salt, pepper, and, if you like, some minced garlic.

Parmigiano-Reggiano

One of the world's oldest and best cheeses, perhaps Italy's most famous, Parmigiano dates back to the Etruscans. It's a cow's-milk cheese aged for at least two years, produced in northern Italy, especially around Parma, Reggio Emilia, and Modena. It comes in giant wheels with its name stamped clearly on the rind. If you can't find the original, some Argentinean brands are acceptable substitutes.

Pecorino Romano

A sheep's-milk cheese aged for about eight months, Romano is produced around Rome and Sardinia. Its sharp, rich flavor is stronger than Parmigiano's. Americans like to use it as a table cheese, but most Italians consider it too strong for that purpose.

Ricotta

Soft cheeses like ricotta used to

Preheat oven to 400°F.

Brush the slices of bread with the olive oil. Bake until golden. Remove bread from the oven and rub the whole peeled garlic on one side of the bread.

Toppings

Much of the point of crostini is the topping that accompanies them. Our favorites include smoked mozzarella, chopped fresh tomatoes, chopped black olives, chopped fresh herbs with capers, onion marmalade, roasted red peppers (see page 56), anchovy paste, minced chicken livers, roasted garlic (see the recipe on page 81), white bean spread (see recipe below), and chopped arugula.

Prep time (bread only): 15 minutes
Yield: About 30 slices

White Bean Spread

This traditional spread combines mellow and meaty flavors in a delightful way.

1/4 cup Italian pancetta or bacon, finely chopped
3 tablespoons olive oil
1/3 cup onion, finely diced
1 teaspoon finely chopped garlic
1-1/2 cups cooked white beans
1/4 cup finely diced celery
6 tablespoons finely diced Italian meats
*   (salami, proscuitto ham, etc.)*
Salt and freshly ground pepper to taste

Sauté the pancetta or bacon in the olive oil until light brown. Remove bacon from pan and drain on paper towels. Add the onion to the pan and sauté until soft. Add the garlic and cook for 3 minutes.

In a food processor, puree the bacon, onions, garlic, oil, and beans until smooth. Transfer to a bowl and stir in the celery, meats, and seasonings. Serve with crackers or crostini, or as a dip for raw vegetables.

Prep time: 30 minutes
Yield: 3/4 cup

Carpaccio

Paper-thin slices of raw beef dressed with capers, shallots, and cheese—adventurous fare for a flavor lover.

12 thin, diagonal slices from a round Italian loaf, crust trimmed
2 tablespoons melted butter
12 paper-thin slices raw beef tenderloin
2 tablespoons capers, drained
2 tablespoons minced shallots
3 tablespoons grated parmesan cheese
12 tiny sprigs fresh parsley
12 thin lemon wedges
Freshly ground black pepper
Extra-virgin olive oil

Preheat oven to 350°F.

Place the bread slices on a baking sheet and brush them with melted butter. Bake until golden, about 5 minutes.

Place a slice of tenderloin on each piece of bread. Sprinkle the tenderloin with capers, shallots, and parmesan. Garnish with parsley sprigs, lemon wedges, and a grinding of black pepper. Drizzle a little olive oil over the top.

Prep time: 20 minutes
Yield: 12 servings

be made from the whey left over from other cheese making, but ricotta is now made from either cow's or sheep's milk in facilities all over Italy. Lower in fat than hard cheeses, creamy white with a neutral taste, ricotta is used in cooking and baking. Since it sours quickly, it should be purchased as fresh as possible.

Gorgonzola

This cow's-milk cheese from Lombardy dates back at least to the ninth century. It is produced in northern Italy (around Gorgonzola) and aged two to nine months. Gorgonzola is a blue-veined cheese with a strong bite and a creamy texture. It mellows when cooked.

Fontina

This semi-soft cow's-milk cheese from the Italian Alps is rich, creamy, and redolent of the herbs and grasses in Alpine pastures. Aged 90 to 100 days, fontina is a good table cheese and a smooth-melting cheese perfect for cooking.

MUSHROOMS

A mushroom poking up through the leaves on the forest floor is a small part of the fungal story. Most of the plant is underground, probably stretching for yards in every direction. If you dig around the base of the mushroom, you'll find a network of fine white threads, called the mycelium. *The succulent mushroom above ground is the fruit of this plant.*

Grilled Bread and Herbed Wild Mushrooms

8 thick slices of coarse Italian bread, quartered
1/4 cup extra-virgin olive oil (divided)
2 cloves garlic, finely chopped
1 tablespoon fresh rosemary, finely chopped (or 1-1/2 teaspoons dried)
1 teaspoon fresh sage, finely chopped (or 1/2 teaspoon dried)
Salt and freshly ground pepper to taste
6 large porcini or shiitake mushrooms, quartered
1 teaspoon freshly squeezed lemon juice
1 small bunch arugula, stems discarded

Preheat the oven to 250°F. Toast the bread in the oven for 10 minutes, or until slightly golden but not dry.

In a small bowl, combine 3 tablespoons of the oil with the garlic, herbs, salt, and pepper. Lightly brush the mushroom caps and bread with the herb oil.

Alternately thread 3 mushrooms and 4 slices of bread on a skewer, beginning and ending with bread. Repeat until all pieces are used.

Preheat the broiler or grill. Grill or broil the skewers until golden brown on all sides.

Whisk the lemon juice into the remaining 1 tablespoon of olive oil and season with salt and pepper to taste. Lightly dress the arugula leaves with the dressing. Serve the skewers on the bed of arugula.

Prep time: 15 minutes
Yield: 8 skewers

Deep-Fried Chick-peas

These little pop-in-your-mouth snacks will disappear by the dozen.

3 15-ounce cans chick-peas
1/2 cup all-purpose flour
2 eggs
1-1/2 tablespoons water
1-1/2 cups fine bread crumbs
Vegetable oil for frying

Drain and rinse the chick-peas. Spread on paper towels and blot dry.

Place the flour in a small bowl. In another bowl, beat the eggs lightly with the water. Place the bread crumbs in a third bowl.

Working with a small handful at a time, roll the chick-peas in the flour, place them in a sieve, and shake gently to remove excess flour. Drop them into the egg and stir gently to coat. Remove them with a slotted spoon and drain briefly. Finally, roll them in the bread crumbs to cover lightly. Place on a baking sheet and let stand for 10 minutes.

Heat the oil in a small saucepan until hot but not smoking. Quickly drop a handful of chick-peas into the oil and fry until they are a dark golden brown. Remove with a slotted spoon and drain on paper towels. Repeat until all chick-peas are fried.

Prep time: 30 minutes
Yield: about 6 cups

Mushrooms spread via spores, which appear on the fleshy gills underneath the cap. The largest spores are the size of a speck of dust. If you run your fingers across the gills, you may come away with spores in the form of a fine powder. Every breeze sends millions of spores out over the forest floor.

ROSEMARY

Rosemary should grace every garden, whether for the marvelous sun-warmed fragrance...the graceful, blue-gray, needle-like foliage...or the proof positive (according to folklore) that a woman runs the house.

Medieval herbalists swore that rosemary warded off demons and bad dreams. Contemporary cooks love rosemary's unmistakable flavor with meat and poultry, tomatoes and mushrooms, eggs and cheese.

To preserve fresh rosemary, freeze entire sprigs. Then, when you're ready to cook, run your thumb and index finger down a sprig, removing as many needles as you need.

Focaccia with Caramelized Onions and Rosemary

This delicious bread with savory toppings is becoming popular even outside Italy.

For the dough:
2 medium baking potatoes
1 package active dry yeast
1-1/2 cups warm water
4 cups all-purpose flour
2 teaspoons salt
1/2 teaspoon sugar
1 tablespoon virgin olive oil
1 tablespoon cornmeal

For the topping:
1-1/2 pounds red onions (3 to 4 medium), sliced
5 tablespoons virgin olive oil (divided)
2 tablespoons sugar
1/2 cup vermouth
2 tablespoons fresh rosemary (or 1 tablespoon dried)

Boil the potatoes until tender. Drain, peel, and mash while still warm.

Dissolve the yeast in the 1-1/2 cups warm water.

In a large bowl, combine potatoes, flour, salt, and sugar. Pour in the dissolved yeast and the oil and stir until blended. Cover with a damp cloth and allow to rise in a warm place until doubled in bulk, about 1 hour.

Sauté the onions in 3 tablespoons of the olive oil until soft. Add sugar and cook over moderate heat until caramelized (brown and shiny), about 25 minutes. Add vermouth and cook 3 minutes longer.

Preheat oven to 375°F.

Lightly oil a 9- by 13-inch baking pan with 1 tablespoon of the remaining olive oil. Sprinkle with cornmeal. Dust your hands with flour, roll out the dough, and press it into the pan. Brush the top of the dough with the last tablespoon of oil. Spread the caramelized onion mixture over the dough and sprinkle with rosemary, salt, and pepper.

Bake 45 minutes to 1 hour, or until focaccia is crisp and golden brown.

Prep time: 1 hour 20 minutes + 1 hour rising time
Yield: 8 servings

Fried Green Tomatoes with Basil

Italians have been eating tomatoes this way for centuries.

4 large green tomatoes, sliced
Salt and freshly ground pepper
12 to 15 fresh basil leaves
3/4 cup all-purpose flour
3 eggs
3/4 cup cornmeal
1 to 2 tablespoons olive oil
1 lemon, cut into wedges

Preheat oven to 250°F.

Drain the tomato slices well on paper towels and season with salt and pepper. Place a basil leaf on each slice.

Place the flour in a small bowl. In a second bowl, mix the eggs with 1 tablespoon water. Place the cornmeal in a third bowl.

Holding the basil leaf on the tomato slice, dip each slice into the flour, then into the egg mixture, and finally into the cornmeal mix, coating thoroughly.

Heat a frying pan over medium-low heat. When pan is hot, add 1 tablespoon of the olive oil and several of the tomato slices. Fry until tomatoes are brown and crisp on one side, then turn them over and fry on the other side. Add more oil as necessary. Do not overcook.

Drain on paper towels and keep in the warm oven until all slices are cooked. Serve warm with lemon wedges.

Prep time: 20 minutes
Yield: 8 servings

BASIL

Native to India, Asia, and Africa, basil was considered a sacred herb by the Hindus, who planted it by temple doors. Now that it has found its way into European and American kitchens, it is treated reverently by committed cooks.

Fresh basil is perhaps the most significant herb in Italian cooking. It's the primary ingredient in

Stuffed Squash Blossoms

These huge, golden blossoms make dramatic finger food.

2 ounces proscuitto ham, sliced paper thin and diced
2 ounces shredded mozzarella
Ground white pepper
1/2 cup all-purpose flour
1/4 cup cornstarch
1/2 teaspoon baking powder
3/4 cup ice water
1 tablespoon olive oil
Vegetable oil for frying
1 egg white
12 squash blossoms (from zucchini, for example),
   pistils removed

Combine the ham and mozzarella in a small bowl. Season with white pepper.

Sift together the flour, cornstarch, and baking powder into a large bowl. Gradually pour the ice water into the dry ingredients, stirring with a fork. Add the olive oil and stir. Do not overmix; the batter should be lumpy.

Heat the vegetable oil in a frying pan over medium heat.

Beat the egg white until soft peaks form. Fold the ham-and-cheese mixture into the beaten white. Open the petals of a squash blossom and stuff it with 1 teaspoon of the filling. Repeat with remaining blossoms.

Dip a blossom into the batter and fry immediately in the hot oil until golden, turning once. Drain on paper towels. Continue until all blossoms are cooked. Serve immediately.

Prep time: 45 minutes
Yield: 6 servings

pesto, that spicy green sauce that causes food lovers to cast their eyes to heaven, and it has a remarkable affinity for tomatoes.

Unfortunately, basil loses much of its magic when dried. Happily, it's easy to grow even for non-gardeners. Basil likes sun, well-drained soil, and protection from the wind. It's easily damaged by frost and cold—sow late and harvest early—and is happy when potted. Set the pot in a sunny window and harvest the spicy leaves all year long.

If you have a bumper crop, try preserving some for the winter ahead. Place the fresh leaves in a small jar and add olive oil to cover. The basil will keep for months if covered completely; uncovered leaves will mold.

Thailand

Defining Ingredients

Lemon grass, limes, coconut, cilantro, hot chilies, garlic, fish sauce, tamarind

Thai food is completely distinctive: fresh and flavorful, often fiery hot, often salty-fishy, frequently flavored with citrus (perhaps the source of its "clean tasting" reputation). It varies from very light—fresh shrimp with lemon grass and lime—to sumptuously rich satay sauces of coconut milk and ground peanuts.

True, Chinese influence is apparent. Thai food is stir-fried, steamed, or grilled over charcoal, and the wok is everywhere in evidence. Noodles almost identical to the Chinese version are a national dish. (Perhaps in recognition of their origin, noodles are eaten with chopsticks, while other dishes are eaten with fork and spoon.)

Unlike the Chinese, however, Thai cooks consider it of little consequence whether the ingredients for a stir-fry are cut with precision. They show little inclination to marinate meat before cooking it and no affection for complicated, cornstarch-thickened sauces. And while they may have appropriated Chinese noodles whole, they make this dish uniquely their own, spooning on fish sauce, chili-vinegar

sauce, lime juice, chopped peanuts, and sugar at the table to suit their individual tastes.

India's influence is also clear. The famous curry spice pastes of Thailand owe a debt to India, and the fresh coriander that pervades Thai cooking was brought from India by Portuguese traders in the 16th century. Unlike Indian cooking, Thai food does not rely on dairy products such as yogurt.

Some quintessentially Thai ingredients are relatively unknown outside the country and must be tracked down in Asian markets (see "Distinctive Thai Ingredients"). Others are common worldwide but are used in a distinctively Thai fashion. Cooking Thai will alter forever your concept of "enough garlic." Many a recipe begins, "Fry 10 to 12 cloves of garlic…"

Chili peppers are so characteristic of Thai food that it's hard to believe they are relative newcomers, brought to Thailand by Portuguese traders in the 17th century. Fiery Thai peppers are not widely available, but any small, hot chili will work well. Mexican chilies so closely resemble Thai peppers that serranos are now being grown in Thailand.

Characteristically, a Thai meal involves a delicate balancing of disparate elements—sweet and sour, hot and cool, fried and steamed, fiery-spicy and mellow. But Thais eat all the time—small bites parceled out through the day. Street vendors are everywhere, appearing magically with the crowds at public events or retracing their daily routes through residential neighborhoods, announcing their charcoaled satay or their fresh spring rolls, selling some of the best finger food in the world.

Deep-Fried Cashews with Chilies and Scallions

Every culture seems to consider nuts a fine finger food, especially when boiled, roasted, or fried. In this recipe, the hot chilies mellow when deep-fried, and the fresh scallions are delicious with the nuts.

1/2 pound whole, raw cashews　　　　*1/4 cup thinly sliced scallions*
1/2 cup small, hot, dried red chilies　　*Vegetable oil for deep frying*
Salt to taste

Pour the vegetable oil into a deep fryer, wok, or skillet to about 3 inches. Heat the oil over medium-low heat (325°F).

Fry the cashews about 5 minutes, stirring occasionally, or until they're golden brown.

Lemon grass

This oriental herb has a strong citrus flavor. It has a long, green, grasslike stem and an elongated white bulb. The bulb is the edible part. Sliced crosswise, its concentric rings resemble shallots.

Kaffir limes

While Thais use the kaffir lime—leaves, rind, juice, and pulp—the widely available Persian lime substitutes admirably.

Remove them from the oil with a slotted spoon or mesh scoop and drain on several layers of paper towels.

Now fry the chilies, being careful not to burn them. The safest method is to place them in the mesh scoop or slotted spoon and dip them in the hot oil for 30 seconds at a time. They will darken and begin to smell roasted. Drain well and place on several layers of paper towels.

Sprinkle the cashews liberally with salt and place them on a serving plate. Arrange the chilies over the nuts and sprinkle the green onions on top.

Prep time: 10 minutes
Yield: 4 servings

Shrimp with Lemon Grass

The citrus flavors of lemon grass and lime juice complement the shrimp in this recipe.

1 stalk lemon grass
1 small shallot
2 serrano peppers
2 tablespoons freshly squeezed lime juice

1 tablespoon fish sauce
1-1/2 teaspoons sugar
1/2 pound shrimp, peeled, with tails left on
Handful fresh mint leaves

Remove the tough outer leaves from the lemon grass, trim off the root end, and cut into a smooth stalk about 3 inches long, measuring from the root end up. Slice crosswise into very thin circles and separate into rings. Peel the shallot, slice it crosswise into thin circles, and separate it into rings. Slice the peppers into thin circles. Stir together the lime juice, fish sauce, and sugar, dissolving the sugar completely.

Cook the shrimp in a little water, simmering gently below the boiling point just until they turn pink, about 2 minutes. Shrimp should be somewhat undercooked; the lime juice will continue to "cook" them. Drain shrimp and combine with all remaining ingredients, mixing well. Let stand 1/2 hour before serving. If desired, spoon a tablespoon of the mix at a time into small, well-curled lettuce leaves for serving.

Prep time: 20 minutes + 30 minutes rest time
Yield: 4 servings

Fish sauce

A thin brown liquid brewed from fish and salt, fish sauce (nam pla) is to Thais what soy sauce is to the Chinese: a principal cooking ingredient and a table condiment added to just about anything that needs more salt or body. Not surprisingly, it is salty and fishy, yet the good ones are neither heavy nor overwhelming.

Tamarind

Inside the seedpods of the tamarind tree is a dark brown pulp with a citrusy, sour flavor. Neatly wrapped blocks of the sticky pulp are available in oriental markets. To make tamarind liquid, break off about 1-1/2 ounces of pulp—about a golf ball and a half—pour 1 cup of boiling water over it, and mash it with a fork. Allow to stand for at least 30 minutes, then strain the liquid and discard the pulp.

If tamarind is unavailable, you can make a tolerable substitute by stirring 3 tablespoons of fresh lime juice into 1 tablespoon of molasses.

Curry Pastes
Small cans of these flavorful concoctions are available at oriental markets, usually identified by color. Leftovers freeze well.

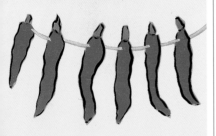

USING HOT CHILIES

Chilies are literally too hot to handle. Prolonged contact between peppers and bare hands can leave you with second-degree chemical burns

70

Soft Spring Rolls

Originally a Vietnamese invention, the wrappers for these delicate rolls are paper-thin rice papers, available at oriental markets.

3 cups assorted vegetables cut into shoestrings: carrots, seeded cucumbers, mushrooms, red or green bell peppers, scallions, and/or sprouts
1 teaspoon minced fresh ginger

1 tablespoon vegetable oil
1 cup Chinese cabbage, cut into long, thin shreds
16 rice papers

Quickly stir-fry the shoestring vegetables and ginger in the oil until lightly softened.

One at a time, soften the rice papers in a shallow bowl of warm water. Lay a paper flat on a work surface. On the lower half of the paper, place 2 tablespoons of the vegetable mixture and sprinkle some Chinese cabbage on top. Fold the sides of the rice paper over the vegetables, then tightly roll up from the bottom, making certain that there are no gaps in the sides. Moisten your fingers with warm water and seal the edges. Allow the rolls to stand for a few minutes to set.

If desired, cut the ends of the rolls on the bias before serving to display the colorful vegetables. Serve with Thai Dressing., Tamarind Dipping Sauce, and/or Chili Lime Sauce.

Prep time: 1 hour
Yield: 16 rolls

Chili Lime Sauce

A good sauce for spring rolls and an interesting dip for raw vegetables.

1/2 cup freshly squeezed lime juice (2 to 4 limes)
2 teaspoons palm or brown sugar

1 to 2 teaspoons minced hot green chili
1 teaspoon minced shallot
1/2 teaspoon fish sauce

In a small bowl, stir lime juice and sugar until sugar has dissolved. Stir in remaining ingredients. Serve with fresh vegetables or spring rolls.

Prep time: 20 minutes
Yield: about 2/3 cup

Damian's Thai Dressing

While this dressing calls for srirachi sauce, a hot oriental specialty, you can substitute Tabasco with excellent results.

1/2 cup lemon juice
2 tablespoons fish sauce
1/3 cup rice wine vinegar
1/2 teaspoon sugar
1/2 teaspoon salt
1-1/2 teaspoons minced garlic
1-1/2 teaspoons minced fresh ginger

1-1/2 teaspoons minced jalapeño pepper
1/4 cup finely chopped cilantro
1/4 cup finely chopped fresh basil
1/2 cup coconut milk
2 tablespoons flaked, unsweetened coconut
2 tablespoons sriracha sauce (or Tabasco)
1 cup vegetable oil

Combine all ingredients except the vegetable oil. Add the oil in a thin stream, whisking constantly until the sauce thickens.

Prep time: 15 minutes
Yield: about 4 cups

Tamarind Dipping Sauce

A good sauce for Spring Rolls or dip for raw vegetables (Thais are fond of fresh green beans). Adjust the proportions to your taste, making it sweeter (more sugar)…saltier (more fish sauce)…more garlicky…or hotter.

1 cup tamarind liquid (see "Tamarind" on page 69)
1 teaspoon palm or brown sugar
1/4 teaspoon fish sauce

2 cloves garlic, minced
1 teaspoon minced hot chili
2 green onions, thinly sliced

Heat tamarind liquid and sugar over low heat until sugar has dissolved. Remove pan from heat and add remaining ingredients. Pour into a serving bowl and allow to cool.

Prep time: 15 minutes
Yield: 1 cup

and hands that feel sensitive and raw for days. If capsaicin—the substance that makes hot peppers hot—gets in your eyes, nose, or any other sensitive area, it will cause searing pain. Capsaicin is not water-soluble, so it's hard to wash off.

If you can tolerate a bit of clumsiness, wear rubber gloves when handling hot chilies. If gloves are a problem, try oiling your hands first. NEVER touch your eyes while handling the peppers.

If your hands burn, try rinsing them with a weak solution of household bleach and water. If chilies burn your mouth, try pop, beer, water, tortillas, bread, or even sugar.

Cleaning Fresh Chilies

Cut away the stem end with a sharp knife and slit the pepper lengthwise. With the knife point, scrape out the seeds and cut out the white, fleshy membranes.

Note: In a burst of machismo or machisma, some cooks recommend that you leave the

71

seeds and veins, since they are thought to contain much of the chili's heat. We think the seeds and veins are less than attractive and that if you want to prove how much heat you can stand, you should just add more peppers.

COCONUTS

Although packaged flaked coconut is widely available, fresh coconuts are delicious and assailable.
Here are a few hints.

Buying

You can judge the freshness of a coconut by its heft; the liquid inside a fresh one makes it heavy. Shake it and listen for the sound of sloshing; a dry coconut is an old coconut. Avoid coconuts with cracked shells; admitted air will cause the flesh to rot.

Opening

Either borrow a chain saw or begin by piercing the "eyes" with a skewer or an icepick.

Shrimp with Coconut

This marvelously strong-flavored dish is typically Thai.

For the base:
1/2 cup dried coconut, shredded
3/4 cup dried shrimp
1/2 cup minced fresh ginger
1 lime, peeled, seeded, and chopped
3 red chili peppers, seeded and thinly sliced

For the sauce:
1 tablespoon shrimp paste
1 cup dried, shredded coconut
1/4 cup ground unsalted peanuts
1/4 cup light brown sugar
1/4 cup fish sauce

Firm inner romaine leaves.

To prepare the base:

Soak the dried coconut in cold water to cover for 10 minutes. Drain. In a skillet on low heat, toast 1/2 cup of the coconut until light brown. In a bowl, combine the toasted coconut, dried shrimp, ginger, lime, and peppers. Set aside.

To prepare the sauce:

In a saucepan over medium heat, combine all sauce ingredients and cook until syrupy, about 10 minutes. Cool slightly.

To assemble:

Place a heaping teaspoonful of the dried shrimp mixture in the center of each lettuce leaf. Top with 1/2 teaspoon of the slightly warm sauce.

Prep time: 45 minutes
Yield: 12 servings

Galloping Horses

It is unclear how these snacks resemble horses or why they appear to gallop, but they are delicious and very popular in Thailand. Thais are justifiably proud of their fruit, especially their pineapples, which they believe are the sweetest in the world.

2 cloves garlic, finely chopped
1 shallot, finely chopped
2 teaspoons vegetable oil
1/2 pound ground pork
2 tablespoons fish sauce
2 tablespoons brown sugar
1/2 teaspoon freshly ground black pepper
3 tablespoons fresh cilantro, chopped
1/4 cup roasted, unsalted peanuts, coarsely chopped
1 fresh pineapple
2 red serrano chilies or other red chili, cut into strips
Small leaves of fresh cilantro, for garnish

Saute the garlic and shallot in the oil until golden. Add ground pork and fry until it loses its pink color. Drain off any excess fat. Add fish sauce, sugar, and black pepper and cook, stirring, until all the pork is coated with sauce. Remove from the heat, taste, and add more fish sauce or brown sugar as needed for a pleasing sweet-salty balance. Stir in cilantro and peanuts, and set aside to cool.

Peel and core the pineapple, and cut across it in 1/4-inch-thick slices. Cut each slice into thirds, to make wedges. Place a spoonful of the pork mixture on each pineapple piece and top with a strip of red chili and a cilantro leaf.

Prep time: 45 minutes
Yield: 6 to 8 servings

Drain off the liquid (the coconut water) and taste it; it should be sweet and pleasant. If it's sour and oily, the coconut is rotten.

Heat the coconut in a 350°F oven for 25 minutes; the shell should crack. Tap the shell to loosen it, then hit it a hard blow with a hammer. The white meat should separate easily from the shell. If it doesn't, pry it loose with a sturdy knife.

Grating

Peel the brown skin off the white meat and grate the meat by hand or in a food processor.

73

Coconut milk is not the liquid gurgling around in a fresh coconut; that's coconut water. Milk is extracted from the grated coconut.

Canned coconut milk is available in oriental groceries and large supermarkets; the best brands come from Thailand. The heavy layer at the top of the can is a very rich coconut cream; shake the can well before using.

To make your own, pour 1 cup of boiling water over 1 cup of tightly packed grated coconut—preferably fresh, but you can use packaged unsweetened coconut in a pinch. Cover and let stand at least 1 hour, then drain. (For a richer product, use very hot milk or coconut water.) An average coconut yields about 3 cups of coconut milk.

Coconut milk freezes beautifully. In the refrigerator it keeps about as long as other kinds of milk.

Satay

One of the best-known Thai foods, satay points to Thailand's close culinary ties with India. The rich Thai peanut sauces are truly superb. A cucumber relish balances the richness.

Meat

1 pound lean pork or boned chicken
1/2 cup coconut milk
1 teaspoon fish sauce
1 teaspoon brown sugar

1/2 teaspoon ground cumin
1/2 teaspoon ground coriander
1/2 teaspoon ground turmeric

Slice the pork or chicken into fairly thin strips about 3 inches long and 1 inch wide. Combine the remaining ingredients, add the meat, cover, and refrigerate for at least 2 hours.

Soak small bamboo skewers in water, so that they don't catch fire on the grill. Thread a piece of meat onto each soaked skewer and grill over a charcoal fire or a gas grill until cooked. Serve meat with Peanut Sauce and Cucumber Relish.

Peanut Sauce

1/2 cup coconut milk
2 tablespoons red curry paste
1/2 cup chunky peanut butter
1/2 cup chicken stock

3 tablespoons brown sugar
2 tablespoons tamarind liquid
1 tablespoon fish sauce
1/2 teaspoon salt

Heat the coconut milk over medium heat about 5 minutes, or until it comes to a gentle boil and small beads of oil form on the surface. Stir the curry paste into the milk until it is thoroughly dissolved. Add peanut butter, stock, and sugar, and cook, stirring constantly, until the sauce is smooth. Remove from heat and add remaining ingredients. Allow to cool to room temperature.

Cucumber Relish

1/2 cup vinegar
1/4 cup water
1 cup sugar
1 teaspoon salt

1 small onion, finely diced
1 small carrot, finely chopped
1 medium-sized green cucumber, finely chopped
1 tablespoon finely chopped cilantro

Boil vinegar, water, sugar, and salt in a small saucepan for 1 minute, or until sugar is dissolved. Place the onion, carrot, and cucumbers in a serving bowl and pour the syrup over them. Garnish with chopped cilantro.

Prep time: 1 hour + 2 hours marinating time
Yield: 6 servings

Son-in-Law Eggs

Many cuisines have high respect for the common egg, treating it as a food well worth embellishing. Although this dish is extremely common in Thailand, the origin of its name is obscure (at least to non-Thais).

Sauce
1/4 cup tamarind liquid
(see "Tamarind" on page 69)
3 tablespoons palm or brown sugar
2 tablespoons fish sauce
2 tablespoons water

Eggs
6 shallots, thinly sliced into crosswise rings
6 garlic cloves, thinly sliced
6 eggs, hard-cooked and shelled
Dried red chili flakes
Vegetable oil for deep frying

To make the sauce, combine all ingredients in a small saucepan and heat, stirring constantly, until sugar dissolves. Set aside.

Heat the oil in deep fryer, wok, or skillet over medium heat (350°F) and deep-fry the eggs, turning them occasionally, until they're golden brown and crisp. Drain on paper towels.

Fry the shallots and garlic until brown (about 1 minute). Remove with a slotted spoon and drain on paper towels.

To serve, cut the eggs in half, lengthwise, and place them cut-side-up on a serving plate. Sprinkle with shallot, garlic, and pepper flakes. Spoon sauce over the top.

Prep time: 30 minutes
Yield: 6 servings

France

Defining Ingredients

Wine, cream, eggs, butter, cheese, herbs, garlic, meat stock, mustard, vinegars, smoked fish, capers

For much of the twentieth century, France defined good food for the rest of the Western world. Serious food lovers sought out French restaurants and intrepid ones consumed French cookbooks, searching for the correct technique and the perfect sauce. No professional chef could hope to be taken seriously unless trained, however briefly, "on the Continent."

The hallmarks of French cooking are well known—a battery of exquisite sauces, a subtle hand with herbs, liberal use of butter, cream, and wine. Still, historic regions vary in emphasis and ingredients.

On the north coast, Normandy produces the richest milk, cream, and butter in the country, and its miles of apple orchards supply cider apples, from which Calvados, a fiery apple brandy, is made. Dishes that combine apples, cider, and cream are often labeled "Normande." Brittany—famous for its crepes—is the largest producer of artichokes in Europe, and that prickly vegetable is prominent as appetizer and side dish. Champagne gave us one of the most famous beverages in the world. Alsace, with its political and culinary ties to Germany, feasts on fois gras and pâtés. Ile-de-France, with Paris (and haute cuisine) at its center, is known for its game, mushrooms, strawberries,

ARTICHOKES

■

A standoffish vegetable, the artichoke has spiky leaves to stab your fingers and a fuzzy choke to do exactly what the name implies. Eating an artichoke can be a blood sport.

On the other hand, this prickly member of the thistle family is delicious. It has been grown around the Mediterranean for centuries and is now also widely cultivated in California.

Artichokes are available year round but are at their best in the spring. Look for firm, heavy specimens with tightly closed leaves. The purple spots on some artichokes may be unsightly, but they're just surface blemishes, the result of an untimely

and Brie. Burgundy gave us fine red wine and dishes flavored with it—*coq au vin* and *boeuf bourguignon*—as well as a taste for escargots and Dijon mustard. Bordeaux produces great wines and brandies—cognac and armagnac—as well as truffles. To the south, Provence celebrates the basic ingredients of other Mediterranean regions: tomatoes, peppers, olive oil, herbs, and garlic. Aioli, that delicious, garlicky sauce, hails from Provence.

Perhaps more than specific ingredients, perhaps even more than the techniques that French chefs taught the rest of the world, the French taught us that cooking and eating can be raised to the level of art, that culinary skills are worthy of our closest attention and our most careful study.

Herbed Cheese Spread

Serve this flavorful spread with crackers or thinly sliced and toasted French bread.

2 ounces goat cheese
2 ounces cream cheese, softened
2 tablespoons chopped fresh parsley
2 teaspoons chopped fresh tarragon
   (or 1 teaspoon dried)
Tiny pinch dried dill
Small squeeze lemon juice
Salt and freshly ground pepper to taste

Blend all ingredients in a food processor until smooth, and refrigerate until ready to serve. Set out to soften 1/2 hour prior to serving. Serve with crackers or thin, toasted slices of French bread.

Prep time: 10 minutes
Yield: 2 servings

Artichoke and Aioli Platter

With its sunburst pattern, this is an attractive dish. Aioli is an ancient sauce, dating back to the garlic-loving Romans.

15 cloves garlic
4 egg yolks
2-1/2 cups extra-virgin olive oil
Lemon juice to taste
Salt and freshly ground pepper to taste
4 large artichokes

With a mortar and pestle, crush the garlic with some of the salt to a smooth paste. Transfer to the bowl of a food processor fitted with a steel blade. Add the egg yolks and blend until smooth. With the motor running, slowly add the olive oil. The aioli will thicken gradually. Season to taste with the lemon juice, salt, and pepper.

To prepare the artichokes, boil them in salted water for 45 minutes, or until the bottom leaves can easily be pulled off. Drain and allow to cool. Remove the leaves and set aside. With a sharp knife, cut out the fibrous choke from each artichoke; if necessary, use a spoon to scrape any remaining fibers off the heart and hollow it out slightly.

Place the artichoke hearts on the center of a serving plate, and spoon some aioli into the center of each one. Arrange the artichoke leaves in concentric circles around the hearts.

To eat, dip the fleshy end of an artichoke leaf into the aioli, and use your teeth to scrape the flesh off the leaf. The delicious hearts are entirely edible.

Aioli is also excellent served with other crudités: cooked new potatoes with skins on; blanched vegetables, including carrots, zucchini, green beans, and beets; hard-boiled eggs; ripe tomato wedges; fresh herbs; lettuce hearts.

Prep time: 10 minutes
Yield: 8 servings (about 2-3/4 cup aioli)

cold spell. They don't mar the taste.

To prepare an artichoke, cut off the bottom of the stem. Unless you have really unpleasant dinner guests, snip off the points of the leaves with kitchen shears. Cook the artichoke in boiling water until done, about 30 to 45 minutes. To test for doneness, try to pull off a couple of leaves. If they come off easily, the artichoke is done.

BLANCHING VEGETABLES

For the crispest vegetables on your aioli platter (or any other plate of crudités), blanch them quickly in boiling, salted water for 10 seconds only. Drain them and then plunge them immediately into ice water for 1 minute, to halt the cooking process. Don't let the vegetables linger any longer in their icy bath, or they will become soggy.

CURDS & WHEY

People have been making cheese for at least 4,000 years, using the milk of whatever animal was handy—cow, sheep, goat, horse, water buffalo, or yak.

Cheese takes up a tenth as much space as the milk it is made from, and it doesn't spoil at the lightning speed for which milk is famous. What probably started out as a means of food preservation became one of the most elegant, complex foods in the world.

Cheese Galette

This rich dish makes good use of great French cheeses.

For the filling:
1/2 pound Roquefort or other blue cheese
1/2 pound cream cheese, softened
1/4 cup dry white wine
1/4 cup heavy cream
1 large egg yolk
2 tablespoons all-purpose flour
Salt and freshly ground pepper to taste

For the pastry:
3 cups all-purpose flour
2 tablespoons sugar
1/4 teaspoon salt
3/4 cup (1-1/2 sticks) cold, unsalted butter,
    cut into 1-inch squares
2 large eggs, lightly beaten

For the pastry topping:
1/4 cup sliced blanched almonds, lightly toasted
1 large egg yolk, mixed with 1 tablespoon water

To make the filling:
In the bowl of a food processor fitted with a metal blade, blend the cheeses, wine, cream, egg yolk, and flour until smooth. Season with salt and pepper.

To make the pastry:
In a large bowl, combine the dry ingredients. Using a pastry fork or two sharp knives, cut in the butter until the mixture resembles coarse meal. Stir in the eggs and knead

briefly in the bowl until well combined. Divide the dough in half, shaping each half into a ball. Wrap the balls of dough in plastic wrap and chill for about 1 hour.

On a lightly floured surface, roll each ball into a 10-inch round. Place one crust in a 9-inch tart or cake pan, pressing the dough gently into the corners and against the sides. Spread the filling evenly over the bottom. Sprinkle with the almonds. Fold the edges of the pastry over the filling.

Place the remaining crust on top and crimp the edges to the two crusts, enclosing the filling completely. Brush the top with the egg-water mixture and chill for 30 minutes.

Preheat oven to 400°F.

Bake the galette for 50 minutes, or until golden brown. Allow to stand for 15 minutes. Turn out gently onto a plate, then onto a cooling rack. Cool completely before serving.

Prep time: 1-1/2 hour + 1-1/2 hours chilling time
Yield: 12 to 16 servings

Roasted Garlic

Garlic mellows when it's roasted, retaining its distinctive flavor but losing much of its bite. Its texture becomes smooth and creamy enough to spread with a table knife.

12 whole heads garlic
Extra-virgin olive oil
2 tablespoons fresh thyme (or 1 tablespoon dried)

2 tablespoons fresh rosemary
(or 1 tablespoon dried)
Salt and freshly ground pepper

Preheat oven to 400°F. Line a small baking sheet with foil, leaving enough foil on all sides to fold over the garlic and seal.

Cut off tops of garlic heads to expose the tops of all cloves. Place the heads, cut side up, on the foil-lined cookie sheet. Drizzle with olive oil. Sprinkle each head with thyme and rosemary. Seal foil over the garlic.

Bake for 1 hour. Serve with crusty French bread.

Prep time: 10 minutes   Cooking time: 1 hour   Yield: 12 servings

The original cheese may have resulted when a farmer put some milk in the only bottle available—a calf's stomach—and left it by the fire a little too long. The fourth stomach of a calf produces rennet, an enzyme that causes milk to curdle.

These days, synthesized rennet is added to huge vats of milk, precipitating the curds to the bottom of the vat. After the liquid whey is drained off, the curds are cut into blocks, stacked, salted, and allowed to ripen.

Before they ripen, "green" cheeses taste pretty much the same—bland. The reason Cheddar doesn't taste like mozzarella is that different microbes are used to ripen it.

For centuries people stacked cheese in cool caves to ripen. What the ripe cheese tasted like depended on which microbe happened to live in that particular cave. One microbe dominated the Roquefort caves in France, for example; another inhabited the caves in the Brie region. *Those famous cheeses could be made only in those parts of the world. These days, when scientists can grow just about any microbe they want, any cheese can be made anywhere.*

GARLIC

"The stinking rose," it's often called, which suggests a bit of ambivalence about this robust herb. Roman soldiers on long marches ate it by the handful to enhance their strength and endurance, and it seems to have worked; they endured long enough to establish an

Chick-pea Crepes

Chick-pea flour gives these crepes a nutty flavor that complements savory fillings very well. Both Ratatouille and Monegasque Onions (see recipes below) make excellent fillings.

1/2 teaspoon dried rosemary
2 tablespoons olive oil
1 cup all-purpose flour
1 cup chick-pea flour
1 teaspoon salt
1/4 teaspoon coarsely ground black pepper
1-1/2 cups warm water
Oil for frying

Gently heat the dried rosemary in the olive oil for 2 minutes on very low heat. Set aside to cool for several minutes.

Mix both of the flours with the salt and pepper. Add the water to the flour mixture and beat it with a whisk until smooth. Beat in the rosemary oil. Let batter rest for 20 minutes.

Heat a small, cast-iron skillet or crepe pan on medium heat. Oil lightly. Pour about 1/4 cup batter into the pan, tipping it so the batter spreads out into 6-inch circle. Cook for about 30 seconds, or until the crepe is golden brown on the bottom. Flip the crepe over with a spatula and cook about 10 or 15 seconds. Remove the crepe to a plate. Continue this procedure until the batter is used up. You should have enough batter to make about 12 crepes. To prevent crepes from drying out, cover them with a cloth until ready to use.

To fill the crepes, lay one flat on a work surface. Place a heaping tablespoon of filling toward one edge and roll the crepe up.

Prep time: 15 minutes
Rest time: 20 minutes
Cooking time: 15 minutes
Yield: 12 crepes

Monegasque-Style Onions

These tasty onions make an excellent filling for chick-pea crepes.

1/2 pound small white onions, blanched
in boiling water for 30 seconds,
plunged into a bowl of ice and cold water,
then peeled
1/4 cup virgin olive oil
1 large tomato, peeled, seeded, and chopped fine
1/2 cup white wine vinegar
1/3 cup dried currants
2 sprigs fresh thyme (or 1/2 teaspoon dried)
1 tablespoon finely chopped fresh parsley
1 cup water
1 clove garlic, mashed into a paste
2 tablespoons sugar
Salt and freshly ground pepper to taste

In a large saucepan, sauté the onions in the oil over moderately high heat until browned.

Add all remaining ingredients and bring to a boil. Reduce the heat and simmer until the onions are tender, checking frequently and adding more water, 1/2 cup at a time, as the liquid evaporates. When onions are almost tender, cook over high heat, stirring, until the liquid is reduced to a glaze. Season with salt and pepper to taste and allow to cool.

Monegasque Onions can be made 1 day in advance and kept covered and chilled.

Serve with toasted French bread or use as a filling for chick-pea crepes.

Prep time: 40 minutes
Yield: about 1-1/2 cups

empire, divide Gaul (France) into three parts, and introduce garlic into much of Europe.

Not only is garlic prominent in virtually all the great cuisines of Europe and Asia, but it's a common medicinal herb, widely prescribed for heart disease, high blood pressure, and vampire bites.

Growing your own is easy. Just separate the cloves of a garlic bulb (even a supermarket bulb) and plant them, plump side down, 1 to 2 inches deep and 4 to 6 inches apart. Since garlic tolerates cold and frost, you can plant in early spring or, better still, in the fall, for a bumper crop the following summer.

When buying garlic, select only firm, crisp cloves. Old, dry, yellowed cloves develop a strong off flavor; don't buy in bulk. Store garlic in a cool, well-ventilated place, not in the refrigerator, where it will mildew.

A GOOD FRENCH WINE

When most of us think of Louis Pasteur, we think of milk. In the 1860s, the great French scientist discovered that heating a liquid would destroy harmful microbes and retard spoilage. These days, milk is "pasteurized" as a matter of course, to the great benefit of the public health. When he made his discovery, however, Monsieur Pasteur was studying wine. He developed heat treatment as a means of preserving the national drink without significantly harming its flavor.

Ratatouille

As delightful to pronounce ("rat-uh-TOO-ee") as it is to eat, this mixture of Provencal vegetables is an excellent filling for chick-pea crepes. There are endless ways to prepare ratatouille. This one preserves the taste of each individual vegetable.

2 small eggplants, cubed
Salt
2 tablespoons olive oil (divided)
Freshly ground pepper to taste
1 pound yellow onions (about 2 medium), chopped
1 teaspoon minced garlic
3 zucchini, cubed
1 red bell pepper, cubed
1 green bell pepper, cubed
2 pounds of tomatoes (about 4 large), seeded and chopped
2 tablespoons chopped parsley
2 tablespoons chopped fresh basil
1/2 teaspoon dried oregano
2 tablespoons olive oil

Place the cubed eggplant in a colander, sprinkle with salt, and allow to stand for 20 minutes. Rinse the eggplant, drain, and pat dry. Sauté the eggplant in 1 tablespoon of the olive oil until softened. Season with pepper and transfer it to a large, heavy-bottomed pan. Set aside.

Sauté the onion and garlic in a little olive oil until onion is translucent; add to the pan.

Sauté the zucchini, then the peppers, in a similar fashion, seasoning each with salt and pepper and adding them to the pan.

Add tomatoes and herbs and cook on very low heat for 15 minutes, stirring often to avoid burning.

Prep time: 1 hour
Yield: about 4 to 5 cups

Smoked Salmon Pâté

In a pinch, canned salmon can substitute for the fresh, although the results won't be quite as pleasing. The smoked salmon, however, can't be replaced.

12 ounces fresh salmon
1/2 cup white wine
1/2 cup bottled clam juice
2 tablespoons unsalted butter (divided)
1/4 cup finely minced shallot
8 ounces smoked salmon, cut into thin strips
2 tablespoons fresh lemon juice
2 tablespoons capers, drained
3 lemons, cut in wedges

Rinse the fresh salmon and pat it dry. Place the wine and clam juice in a medium skillet and bring to a boil. Add the fresh salmon, cover, reduce the heat to simmer, and poach for 6 or 7 minutes, or until the fish turns opaque and is easy to pierce with a fork. Drain the fish and discard the liquid. Remove the skin and flake the flesh with a fork. Set aside.

Wipe the skillet dry. Melt 1 tablespoon of the butter and sauté the shallot until soft. Add the smoked salmon and sauté for 2 or 3 minutes, mashing it with the back of a spoon. Remove from the heat and add the flaked fresh salmon, mashing and stirring until the fish are combined.

Beat in the remaining butter and then the lemon juice. Pack the mixture into a crock, cover, and refrigerate for several hours.

To serve, sprinkle the capers over the top of the crock and garnish with the lemon wedges. Spread on crackers or sliced French bread.

Prep time: 45 minutes
Yield: 3 cups

■

Classic French cuisine developed where it could— in aristocratic houses with enough money to support expert chefs and large staffs of assistants. Many a famous concoction is named for a nobleman—or, more accurately, for the noble- man's cook.

The kitchen staff of Louis de Béchameil, one of Louis XIV's courtiers, gave us bechamel sauce. The "Mornay" in the original mornay sauce was the sur- name of a wealthy Huguenot family. Mayonnaise was named for the Minorcan port of Mahon, wrested from the English by the Duc de Richelieu in 1756. Hollandaise sauce was devel- oped by French Huguenots living in Holland.

With the French Revolution in 1789, some noblemen lost

86

Spinach and Ham Tarts

Slices of rye bread make quick and flavorful crusts for these individual tarts.

16 slices rye bread	*1/2 pound boiled ham, cut into 16 slices*
6 tablespoons butter, melted	*1 pound fontina cheese, thinly sliced*
1 pound fresh spinach	*2 eggs*
Salt, freshly ground pepper,	*1-1/2 cups heavy cream*
* and nutmeg to taste*	

Preheat the oven to 375°F.

Cut the crusts off the slices of bread, and flatten them with a rolling pin. Brush the bread on both sides with melted butter. Fit each bread slice into an individual tart pan. Bake for 5 minutes, or until set and lightly golden. Set aside.

Wash the spinach well, towel-dry the leaves, and chop very coarsely. Sauté in the remainder of the melted butter until just wilted. Season with salt, pepper, and nutmeg. Drain.

Spread 1 tablespoon of the chopped spinach on the bottom of each crust. Top with a slice of boiled ham, then 1 or 2 slices of fontina.

Beat the eggs with the heavy cream; season with salt, pepper, and nutmeg. Pour just enough egg mixture into each tart pan to bind the filling together.

Bake until heated through and set, about 15 to 20 minutes. The cheese should just melt and the filling just set. Serve warm.

Prep time: 1 hour
Yield: 16 tarts

Tapenade

This classic dish from Provence takes its name from the French *tapeno*, or "caper." An excellent spread for crackers or bread, tapenade is also a piquant filling for miniature tarts or a topping for broiled poultry and seafood.

1-1/2 tablespoons capers, rinsed and patted dry
6-1/2 ounces high-quality canned tuna,
  packed in oil, undrained
1 anchovy filet, packed in oil
1/2 cup Nicoise olives
1/2 cup pitted dry-cured black French olives with herbs

1 strip lemon zest, minced
1 teaspoon lemon juice
1/4 cup extra-virgin olive oil
1 small garlic clove, chopped
1 tablespoon brandy
Fresh chopped parsley to garnish

Combine all the ingredients except the parsley in a food processor and process very briefly, to create a coarsely textured spread. Serve with lightly toasted slices of French bread. Garnish with chopped parsley.

Prep time: 15 minutes
Yield: About 1-1/2 cups

Anchoiade

If you like anchovies—or just robust flavors in general—this strong-flavored snack will awaken your taste buds.

4 ounces flat anchovy fillets in olive oil,
  drained (reserve the oil)
4 cloves garlic, coarsely chopped
1/3 cup fresh parsley, chopped

2-1/2 teaspoons red wine vinegar
16 slices French bread from baguette,
  cut 1/2 inch thick

Soak the anchovies in 1 cup of cold water for 15 minutes, to remove some of the excess salt. Drain and pat dry.

Preheat the broiler.

Finely chop the anchovies. Add the reserved oil and all remaining ingredients except the bread. The mixture should be rather coarse.

Arrange the bread slices on a baking sheet. Toast under the broiler until crisp and golden on one side.

Turn the bread over and spread the anchoiade on the untoasted sides of bread, pressing it into the bread. Broil for about 1 minute, just until warm. Serve immediately.

Prep time: 15 minutes (+ 15 minutes soaking time)   Yield: 16 pieces

their heads and many more lost their fortunes—two mishaps that produced a great number of unemployed chefs. The result was the "restaurant," from the French restaurer, "to restore."

87

India

Defining Ingredients

*Spices, including cinnamon, cardamom, coriander,
cloves, cumin, chilies, ginger, black pepper,
ground red pepper, turmeric*

Intensely flavorful and amazingly diverse, Indian food
is one of the world's great cuisines. Indian cooks embrace
entire categories of flavors that some cultures seem to
ignore, like artists who insist on working only in cool blues
and greens, blind to hot reds and warm yellows. Indian
dishes may be hot-and-sour, hot-and-sweet, hot-and-nutty,
bitter-and-hot, bitter-and-sour, sweet-and-salty, and a dozen
other combinations.

Of course, Indians have always had a great many flavors
to experiment with. Such well-known spices as cinnamon
and black pepper are native to the Indian subcontinent,
along with dozens more that Westerners still consider exotic
(see "Exotic Indian Spices"). Nutmeg and cloves grew on the
nearby Molucca Islands (the fabled "Spice Islands"). As a
result, when Europeans were eating boiled cabbage and
onions, Indians had developed a skill with spices that led
most of Europe to establish navies, charter East India
companies, and build empires (see "The Spice Trade").

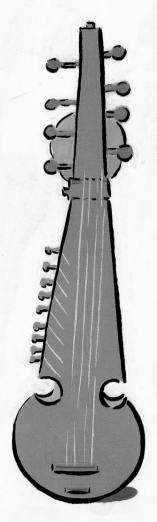

Spices were largely responsible for the rise of England, Portugal, Holland, and France as great maritime powers...for the invention of sea-going navigational instruments...and for the discovery of the New World.

Not bad for a couple of peppercorns.

It's hard to conceive of a world without spices, without even black pepper. Once that is imagined, however, it becomes clear just how valuable spices would be and just how much trouble people would go to in order to get them.

In a pre-refrigerated world, food was difficult to preserve. Not only were spices preservatives, but they helped to mask the off-flavors of partially spoiled food. And they simply made a limited diet taste good.

At least as early as 2000 years B.C., Arab traders were trafficking in Indian

Indians cook with spices in a variety of ways. They use them whole or ground to a powder, serve them raw or roasted. They fry spices in hot oil, then pour both spice and oil over the food just before serving it.

Larger than all of Europe, India includes three main regions: the mountainous north, the rich central plains, and the tropical south. Bounded on the north by the Himalayas, northern India has a temperate climate. Kashmir, the northernmost province, is paradisiacal, with cool air, blue lakes, Persian gardens, walnut groves, and fruit orchards. Sheep thrive in the cool air, and the lamb biryanis of the north are legendary. Bread is the traditional staple, although rice is now eaten everywhere.

Farther south the land becomes flatter and the air warmer. World-famous basmati rice grows in the central plains, along with lentils and an abundance of vegetables.

The tropical south—Goa, Malabar, Maharashtra, Madras—is warm, wet, and humid, and rice is the principal staple. Bananas, coconuts, and dates grow in profusion, and the coastline provides an abundance of shellfish, including shrimp, crab, lobster, clams, and mussels, as well as splendid whitefish. Southern food tends to be very hot, with a great use of mustard oil (as in Madras curry).

Religious diversity has also shaped Indian cooking. Hindus and Sikhs don't eat beef. Muslims and Jews don't eat pork. Buddhists, with their traditional belief in reincarnation, understandably tend toward vegetarianism. Jains and Brahmins are such strict vegetarians that they don't eat vegetables that *resemble* meat (for example, beets and tomatoes, as red as blood). This maze of prohibitions has produced a vegetarian cuisine unequalled in quality and diversity.

Indians are great snackers, and vendors are on every city street corner. Some of the tidbits they sell are included in the recipes below. Other recipes are for dishes more likely to be encountered in an Indian home.

Pappadams

These lentil wafers are among the easiest Indian snacks to prepare. Made of a "dough" of beans that have been ground to a paste and then kneaded, pappadams are available in Indian markets and specialty-food stores.

Lentil wafers
Vegetable oil

Fill a frying pan or deep fryer with oil to a depth of 1-1/2 inches and heat the oil to medium hot (350 to 375°F). Grasp a wafer with tongs and slip it into the oil. Fry for 3 to 5 seconds, using the tongs to keep the wafer submerged. It will expand to double its original size. Lift it out, shake it gently over the pan to remove excess oil, and place it on a cookie sheet covered with several layers of paper towels.

Pappadams may be fried ahead of time and set aside. Just before serving, reheat, uncovered, in a medium-hot oven for 2 minutes.

Cooking time: 10 to 15 minutes

Samosas

Perhaps the most famous Indian finger food, these spicy little pies deserve their international reputation.

Pastry
1-1/2 cups all-purpose flour
1/2 teaspoon salt
4 tablespoons vegetable oil
4 to 6 tablespoons cold water

Sift the flour and salt together into a large bowl. Add the oil and rub it into the flour with your fingers until the mixture resembles coarse bread crumbs. Add the cold water and mix. Gather the dough in your hands; it should hold together in a ball. If it doesn't, add a few more drops of cold water.

Knead the dough for 10 minutes, until it is firm but pliable. Rub the surface with a little oil, cover the dough with a towel, and allow it to rest for half an hour. (The dough can be made a day ahead of time and refrigerated, tightly covered. Remove from refrigerator half an hour before using.)

spices. For centuries they dominated the spice trade, sailing to India and the Molucca Islands, returning with cinnamon, cloves, nutmeg, and other exotica. To discourage competition, they spread rumors about their sources. Cinnamon, they said, grew in shallow lakes guarded by winged monsters. Pepper trees grew in deep forests infested with poisonous snakes.

By the early 13th century, Venice had wrested control of the spice trade from the Arabs. Venetian traders acted as middlemen, buying spices in the East and selling them to the rest of Europe.

The rest of Europe chafed under Venetian monopoly of

an incredibly lucrative trade. In the 15th century, they determined to go get their own, and they built the fleets of ships required for the voyage. The explorers familiar to every schoolchild—Columbus, John Cabot, Magellan, Sir Francis Drake—sailed in search of spices. The British occupation of India and the Dutch occupation of Indonesia resulted from cinnamon, cardamom, and cloves.

Filling

5 medium potatoes
4 tablespoons vegetable oil
2 teaspoons coriander seeds
1/2 cup finely chopped onions
1-1/2 teaspoons minced fresh ginger

2 small, hot green chilies, seeded and chopped
3/4 cup frozen green peas, thawed
1-1/4 teaspoons garam masala (see recipe below)
1 tablespoon lemon juice
Salt to taste

Boil the potatoes until soft. Peel and cut into 1/4-inch cubes.

Place the oil in a medium skillet and heat over medium-high heat until hot but not smoking. Add the coriander seeds and fry until they brown (about 15 seconds). Add onions, ginger, and chilies, and fry until the onions turn light brown (4 to 5 minutes). Add potatoes and peas, stir to coat with oil, and continue frying until peas are done and potatoes look dry and "fried," about 10 minutes. Add remaining ingredients, cook 3 or 4 minutes, and set aside. (The filling can be made beforehand and refrigerated until ready to use.)

Assembly and cooking:

Knead the dough again briefly and divide it in half. Divide each half into 8 pieces and shape each piece into a ball. Dust a ball with flour and roll it into a 6-inch circle. Cut the circle in half. Repeat with remaining dough.

Form each semicircle into a cone by folding it in half along the straight edge and overlapping the two edges by about 1/4 inch. Moisten the seam with a little water and press the overlapped edges together securely to seal.

Place a tablespoon or so of filling in the cone. Moisten the open end of the cone and pinch it shut, making a triangular shape. Make sure all edges are tightly sealed; openings will allow oil to seep into the filling during frying and make the filling greasy.

Samosas can be made a few hours before cooking. If the pastry dries a little, they will only become crisper when fried.

Heat 1-1/2 to 2 inches of oil in a deep fryer or large skillet over medium-low heat and fry the samosas a few at a time until golden brown (about 10 to 12 minutes). Remove from the oil with a slotted spoon and drain on paper towels. Serve hot, warm, or at room temperature.

Prep time: 1-1/2 hours
Cooking time: 30 to 40 minutes
Yield: 32 samosas

Garam Masala

There are as many recipes for this wonderful spice mixture as there are cooks in India. Adjust the mixture to suit your own tastes. Used constantly in Indian cooking, garam masala is added to the dish a few minutes before it finishes cooking.

A different style of garam masala includes ground coriander instead of nutmeg. However, since many Indian recipes specify adding both the masala and some ground coriander, this recipe is the more versatile of the two.

The spices in garam masala do not have to be roasted.

1 tablespoon cardamom seeds
2-inch piece stick cinnamon
1 teaspoon cumin seeds
1 teaspoon whole cloves
1 teaspoon black peppercorns
1/2 teaspoon ground nutmeg

Grind everything but the nutmeg in a spice grinder or coffee grinder until the spices are finely ground (often a full minute). Stir in the ground nutmeg. Store in a small container with a tight-fitting lid, away from heat.

Prep time: 5 minutes
Yield: about 1/4 cup

EXOTIC INDIAN SPICES

Although some Indian spices are popular worldwide—cinnamon and black pepper, for example—others are less familiar.

Turmeric

Like ginger, turmeric is a rhizome that grows underground, jutting out horizontally from the root. A perennial herb with a woody aroma, turmeric is native to India and used throughout the country, mostly for the rich, yellow color it dyes whatever it's cooked with. Turmeric is the main ingredient in commercial curry powder.

Black mustard seeds

An annual herb, black mustard is native to India and is one of the most important spices throughout the country. The purplish brown seeds are bitter when raw but become sweeter and mellow when roasted or fried in hot oil until they pop.

Cardamom

Native to southern India and Sri Lanka, cardamom is incredibly fragrant. The whole pods will fill your kitchen with their sweet, exotic scent. Green cardamom pods are 1/4 to 1/2 inch long. The black variety has pods about 1 inch long;

Kashmiri Kebabs

Not all kebabs are skewered. These miniature meatballs use the ground lamb and the luxurious spices of the north.

Meatballs:
1/2 cup yellow split peas (chana dal)
1/4 cup chopped onion
1 tablespoon finely chopped fresh ginger
8 whole green cardamom pods
6 cloves
2 inches stick cinnamon
2 bay leaves
Salt to taste
1 pound lean ground lamb or beef

Filling:
2/3 cup fresh mint leaves
2/3 cup cilantro leaves
2 to 3 small, hot chilies, chopped
1/3 cup raisins
Grated rind of 1 lemon and 1 orange

Assembly and cooking:

Rinse the chana dal and place it in a saucepan, along with the onion, ginger, spices, bay leaves, and 1 cup water. Simmer until the dal is tender (about 1 hour), checking to see that it doesn't burn and adding a little more water if necessary. Drain well of any excess liquid. Remove spices and bay leaves, and puree the dal in a food processor. Add salt to taste.

Mix the puree into the ground meat, working it in with your hands until thoroughly blended. Refrigerate until ready to cook. (The kebab mixture can be prepared a day ahead and refrigerated.)

Place all filling ingredients in a food processor and grind into a coarse paste.

Divide meatball mixture and filling mixture into 20 equal portions. Divide each meatball portion in half and shape each half into a flat, oval patty. Lay a row of filling down the middle of one half, top it with the other half, and crimp the edges together. Flatten the entire patty slightly.

Cover the bottom of a skillet with a thin film of oil and fry the kebabs until done. Or, if you prefer, place them on a rack and broil them until done.

Serve with any of the chutneys.

Prep time: 1 hour + 1 hour simmering for dal
Yield: 20 kebabs

Pakoras

Pakoras are delectable little morsels—small pieces of vegetables dipped in a chick-pea-flour batter and deep fried. There are countless recipes for pakora batters. We've included two: one spicy and one hot version.

Good vegetables for pakoras include cauliflower (separated into florets); zucchini (cut 1/4 inch thick); onions, potatoes, sweet potatoes, eggplant, and plantains (peeled and sliced 1/4 inch thick); spinach leaves (washed and patted dry).

Pakora Batter I
1 cup chick-pea flour
1/4 teaspoon baking soda
1/2 teaspoon salt
3/4 to 1 cup water
1/2 teaspoon turmeric
1/2 teaspoon cayenne

Pakora Batter II
1 cup chick-pea flour
1/8 teaspoon cloves
1/2 teaspoon cayenne
1 teaspoon ground coriander
1/2 teaspoon ground cardamom
3/4 cup water

Combine all batter ingredients and whisk until smooth.

Pour vegetable oil into a skillet, wok, or deep fryer to a depth of 2 inches. Heat the oil on medium heat (350°F).

Dip several vegetable pieces in the batter and drop them gently into the hot oil. Fry, turning once, until golden, about 7 minutes.

Cooking times will vary with the vegetable. Eggplant should be cooked through, for example, but cauliflower can keep a little of its crunch. Flowers and spinach leaves cook quickly; save them until last.

When each batch of pakoras is cooked, remove with a slotted spoon and drain on paper towels.

Prep time: 15 minutes
Yield: about 2 cups batter

they have a mellower taste but are much harder to find outside of India. Depending on the recipe, you can season a dish with either the whole pods or the tiny black seeds inside.

Coriander

Coriander seeds look like small, pale peppercorns. They are the dried fruit of the coriander plant—that is, fresh cilantro. They have a strong aroma and sweetish taste, and they improve with roasting. Coriander is an indispensable Indian spice.

Fennel

Native to the Mediterranean but cultivated in India for centuries, fennel seeds impart a sweet licorice flavor to a variety of dishes.

TANDOOR

The skewered "tandoori" shrimp and meats served by most Indian restaurants are named for the tandoor, originally a clay pit with a fire in the bottom, then a hot clay oven. Bread was smacked onto the side of the pit, where it baked and absorbed the earthy aroma of the clay. Seafood and meats were marinated in spiced yogurt to tenderize them, then threaded onto long skewers and lowered into the pit. Tandoori foods are bright red-orange, colored by a spice added to the marinade.

Barbecued Shrimp

These spicy shrimp are excellent for nibbling.

1 pound raw, peeled shrimp
1/4 cup vegetable oil
1/2 small onion, minced
1 tablespoon finely chopped mint leaves
1 teaspoon finely chopped fresh basil,
    or 1/2 teaspoon dried
2 cloves garlic, crushed
1 teaspoon paprika
1/4 teaspoon cayenne
1 teaspoon freshly ground black pepper
1/4 teaspoon salt
1-1/2 tablespoons vinegar
1-1/2 teaspoons turmeric
Wooden skewers, soaked in water

Wash and devein the shrimp and pat them dry. Combine the remaining ingredients and marinate the shrimp 8 to 10 hours, or overnight.

Place shrimp on skewers and grill over hot coals, basting with marinade once or twice and being careful not to overcook them.

Prep time: 20 minutes
Marinating time: overnight
Cooking time: 5 to 6 minutes
Yield: 4 servings

Coconut and Green Chili Chutney

A world-famous Indian creation, chutneys are eaten with practically anything that needs a contrasting flavor or a little extra moisture. Mango chutney is the classic, but Indians rely on seasonal fruits and herbs.

3 cups fresh minced coconut (or 3 cups unsweetened flaked coconut)
1 cup yogurt
2 small, hot, green chili peppers, seeded, deveined, and minced
1 tablespoon minced fresh ginger
1 tablespoon sugar
1 teaspoon salt
3 tablespoons sesame oil
1-1/2 teaspoons black mustard seeds
1/2 teaspoon ground cumin

Combine coconut, yogurt, peppers, ginger, sugar, and salt.

Heat oil in small skillet over medium-high heat. Add mustard seeds, cover, and cook until seeds pop (about 1-1/2 minutes). Add the cumin, stir quickly, and immediately remove from heat. Pour the oil and spices over the coconut mixture and stir well.

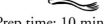

Prep time: 10 minutes
Yield: about 4 cups

Walnut Chutney

2/3 cup shelled walnuts
1/4 teaspoon salt
1/2 teaspoon cayenne
1/4 cup plain yogurt

YOGURT

An indispensable ingredient in Indian cooking, yogurt serves as meat tenderizer, sauce thickener, flavor enhancer, and a creamy counterpoint to hot and spicy food. Indian yogurt is thick, sweet, and rich. Some cooks recommend that if you're limited to American yogurt, you should use a mixture of three-quarters yogurt and one-quarter sour cream for Indian dishes.

A fine but little-known ingredient is yogurt "cheese." To make this thick, creamy product, line a funnel or strainer with several layers of cheesecloth and prop it over a jar or bowl. Place the yogurt in the strainer. (Don't use yogurt that's been stabilized with gelatin or vegetable gum; the whey won't drain out.) Up-end a plastic bag over the whole contraption and refrigerate overnight.

Roasting spices is a characteristically Indian method of getting even more variety from an extensive spice cabinet. Roasted spices simply taste different—richer, mellower—and Indians prefer them in certain dishes.

To roast spices, heat a heavy skillet (preferably cast iron) over medium heat until it's hot. Add the spices and roast, stirring and shaking the pan constantly to prevent scorching. The spices will steam,

Place walnuts, salt, and cayenne in a mortar and grind, pound, and work until the walnuts are smooth. (Or use a food processor or coffee grinder to reduce the nuts almost to a paste.) Place the nut mixture in a bowl and stir in the yogurt.

Prep time: 15 minutes
Yield: about 3/4 cup

Peach Chutney

A native of China, the peach was introduced into northern India by the Moghuls, whose reign saw some of the highest development of Indian cuisine.

2 to 2-1/4 pounds fresh peaches
2 cups white vinegar
1 pound sugar
1 teaspoon salt
1 teaspoon crushed red pepper
1 garlic clove, minced
1/2 cup raisins
2 ounces crystallized ginger, chopped fine

Wash the peaches but do not peel them. Cut them into chunks and place them in a large saucepan. Add the vinegar, sugar, and salt, bring to a slow boil, and boil for 45 minutes. Remove the fruit and reserve it. Boil the liquid another 45 minutes, skimming the foam as necessary. Add the pepper flakes and minced garlic and continue to boil until the liquid starts to thicken. Return the peaches to the pan. Add the raisins and cook another 30 minutes. Remove from the heat and stir in the ginger. Store in the refrigerator.

Prep time: 20 minutes
Cooking time: 2-1/2 hours
Yield: 2 to 4 cups

Green Mango Pickles

No self-respecting house is without a jar of mango pickles, ready to top any snack that needs an extra kick.

2 raw green mangoes
1/3 cup minced fresh ginger
2 teaspoons salt
1 teaspoon cayenne
3 tablespoons light sesame oil
1-1/2 teaspoons black mustard seed

Rinse the mangoes and wipe completely dry. (Water left on the surface will spoil the pickles.) Cut the unpeeled mango into 1/2-inch cubes and place in a small bowl. Add the ginger, salt, and cayenne, and stir to mix well.

Heat the oil in a frying pan until very hot. Add the mustard seeds and fry them until they pop. Pour the oil and seeds over the mango and mix well. Let stand at least 1/2 hour before serving. Refrigerate any leftovers.

Prep time: 20 minutes + 30 minutes rest time
Yield: about 2-1/2 cups

then turn incredibly fragrant, then begin to brown. Once they start to brown, they will burn quickly; watch them carefully.

Times vary with each batch of spices, but generally 1/4 cup of coriander seeds will take about 6 minutes; 1/4 cup of cumin seeds will take about 8 minutes.

When the spices are done, remove them immediately from the pan and place them in a bowl to cool. Grind them to a fine powder in a spice mill or coffee grinder, or pulverize them with a mortar and pestle.

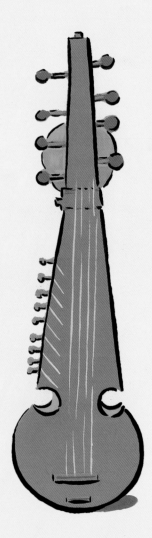

Parathas

Flaky and crisp on the outside, soft on the inside, these fragrant breads are wonderful warm by themselves or with meat, seafood, or vegetable snacks.

1-3/4 cups whole wheat flour
1-3/4 cups all-purpose flour
1/2 teaspoon salt
2/3 cup melted butter
About 1 cup warm water

Place the flours and salt in a medium bowl. Sprinkle 2 tablespoons of melted butter over the flour and rub the butter into the flour with your fingers, until the mixture resembles coarse bread crumbs. Slowly add the water. Gather the flour up into a soft ball.

Knead the dough for about 10 minutes; the dough should be smooth and soft, but not sticky. Shape the dough into a ball and rub a thin film of butter over the surface. Place it in a plastic bag and set aside for at least 1/2 hour.

Preheat a large, cast-iron skillet or griddle over medium-low heat. Meanwhile, knead the dough briefly again and divide it into 12 equal balls. Keep the balls covered until you're ready to work with them.

Flatten a ball of dough and dust it lightly with white flour. Roll it out into a 6-inch round, dusting your work surface with flour if necessary. Brush 1/4 teaspoon butter over the surface and fold the round in half. Spread another 1/4 teaspoon butter over the surface and fold in half again, to form a triangle. Roll the dough out until it forms a larger triangle, 6 to 7 inches on each side.

Brush the hot frying pan with butter and place the paratha in the pan. Cook for about 1 minute, then brush the top with butter. Turn it over and cook the second side for about 1 minute. Both sides should have dark gold spots.

Place the cooked paratha on a plate and cover with foil while the remaining ones are cooked.

Prep time: 40 minutes + 30 minutes resting time
Yield: 12 parathas

Banana Pooris

Pooris are recreational bread: air-filled balloons of golden brown dough. When fried, the flat rounds of dough inflate into spheres. The subtle banana flavor of these pooris works well with savory Indian dishes. For a sweet snack, sprinkle the hot pooris with powdered sugar and serve hot. The banana flavor is more apparent when the pooris are sugared.

1 very ripe banana
1/2 cup cake flour
3/4 cup all-purpose flour

1-1/2 tablespoons oil (divided)
Confectioner's sugar (optional)
Vegetable oil for deep frying

Mash the banana well, using a potato masher, blender, or food processor. You should have 4 about tablespoons of banana puree.

Sift both flours into a bowl. Add 1 tablespoon of the oil and rub it into the flour until the mixture resembles bread crumbs. Add 1 to 2 tablespoons water and form the dough into a ball. Knead for about 10 minutes; the dough will be very stiff.

Shape the dough into a ball. Rub it with a little oil, place it in a plastic bag, and set it aside for about 1 hour.

Knead the dough briefly once more, and divide it into 8 equal parts. Keep the portions you're not working with covered with plastic wrap.

Heat 2 to 3 inches of oil in a wok or deep fryer over medium heat (375°F). Meanwhile, lightly flour your work surface. Form one piece of dough into a ball, flatten it, and roll it out evenly with a rolling pin until you have a thin disk 4-1/2 to 5 inches in diameter.

To fry the poori, lay one flat on top of the hot oil. (If the poori sinks and stays on the bottom, the oil isn't hot enough.) Using a slotted spoon, gently tap the poori to keep it submerged, being careful not to fold it. When it balloons and turns golden on the bottom, turn it over and fry it on the other side for a few seconds. Remove from the oil and drain on paper towels.

Prep time: 40 minutes
Yield: servings

SPAIN

Defining Ingredients

*Olives and olive oil, almonds, garlic, red peppers
both sweet and hot, tomatoes, fish and seafood.*

S panish food is defined less by a single flavor than by
a dominant color: a blazing red-orange. Like many other
elements of Spanish cuisine, the tomatoes and roasted
peppers that color it arrived from somewhere else.

Everybody who is anybody has invaded Spain. The
Phoenicians, the Greeks, the Carthaginians, and the
Romans came early and often. Perhaps most significantly,
the Moors—Arabic people from North Africa—crossed the
narrow Strait of Gibraltar in 711 and stayed, dominating
architecture, art, and food for seven centuries. (Even one-
third of Spanish words are Arabic in origin.) All have contributed to the flavor of Spain. The Romans brought their
beloved grapevines and olive trees. Today, the vines produce
the renowned Spanish sherry in the southern region of
Andalucia and the famous red wines of Rioja in the northeast. The gnarled, long-lived olive trees thrive in the parched
clay soil of Andalucia. On giant plantations, legions of gray-

green olive trees march in formation across the terra-cotta earth. Spain is a leading exporter of olive oil, producing a version that is especially flavorful and fruity.

The Moors introduced melons, sugar cane, nutmeg, and black pepper, and planted huge groves of orange and lemon trees. Now, in the Levant in the east, the citrus groves stretch for miles. More importantly, the Moors brought saffron, that indispensable flavor of paella, the national dish of Spain. The most expensive spice in the world, saffron strands are the stigmas of crocus flowers. Today, purple fields of saffron crocus bloom across the central tablelands of New Castile.

The Moors also planted enormous groves of almond trees, which still cover hillsides in the southeast. Almonds are prominent in Spanish cooking—roasted as a finger food, chopped as a topping, or ground as a thickener for sauces. The city of Toledo gave us marzipan (from the Arabic *mawthapan*), that supreme almond-lover's confection.

Spain's invasions of other continents added to the national cuisine. When the Conquistadors returned from subduing much of Central and South America, they brought back tomatoes, peppers, and potatoes.

Regions

Although it's possible to speak of a distinctively Spanish cuisine, the various regions of Spain are alive and well. Food has a highly regional flavor.

With both Mediterranean and Atlantic coasts, there is an abundance of seafood, and Spaniards consume it with gusto. Inland, fertile valleys grow fresh produce. Navarra, in the north, is renowned for its tomatoes, its peppers, and its fat asparagus. Spain is the leading supplier of asparagus for all of Europe.

In the northeast, Catalonia, which stairsteps up from the Mediterranean to the Pyrenees, is known for its roasted red peppers and its wild mushrooms. In the fall, gatherers sell them by the side of the road in sizes ranging from dinner plates to thimbles. Catalan sauces are known the length and breadth of the country, including *sofrito*, which consists of slow-cooked tomatoes and onions, and the wonderful *romesco* sauce, named for the small red peppers that flavor it.

From the windswept tablelands of the interior comes a fondness for sausages, especially *chorizo*, fragrant with garlic and paprika. Eggs are taken seriously and considered worthy of a treatment all their own.

Tapas

Perhaps Spain's most delightful contributions to the world of food are *tapas*—small tidbits served with drinks. Tapa means "lid," or "cover," and the usage probably derives from an earlier custom of serving a glass of sherry with a piece of bread on top to keep out dust and flies.

Tapas can range from the deliciously simple—a bowl of olives or roasted almonds, fresh mushrooms sautéed in olive oil and garlic and stacked on a wooden skewer—to the exquisitely complex. Often they are just small portions of a dish that would otherwise be part of the meal—squares of Spanish omelette, for example.

Tapas have been the salvation of many a hungry traveler starving to death in a country that adores food. Typically, Spaniards eat a light breakfast, take a late-morning snack break at 11:00, and eat a substantial midday meal at 2:00. Dinner is normally at 10:00 or later. Happily for the tourist accustomed to a noon lunch and a 6:00 dinner, taverns serve tapas at about those times.

Simple tapas usually include regional seafood: fried fresh anchovies and broiled seasnails in Andalucia, fried fresh sardines in Catalonia, sardines and tiny freshwater eels in the Basque provinces of the north, edible barnacles *(percebes)* in the northwestern province of Galicia. Although these aren't available everywhere, equally delightful Spanish tapas can be concocted in virtually any home.

Marinated Olives

It's hard to imagine a tapas table without a bowl of olives. Marinated in the herbs of your choice, they become even more interesting and flavorful.

7-ounce jar manzanilla olives
3 cloves garlic, crushed
1 large bay leaf
1/2 teaspoon oregano
1/4 teaspoon rosemary

1/2 teaspoon ground cumin
1/2 teaspoon fennel seed
1/2 teaspoon thyme
4 tablespoons white vinegar

Drain brine from jar and rinse olives under running water. Set aside. Place remaining ingredients in olive jar, return the olives, and fill to the brim with water. Cap jar and shake. Marinate at room temperature at least 2 days before serving.

Prep time: 10 minutes

105

Potato Omelette

In Spain, a "tortilla" is not the flat, unleavened bread of Mexico, but an omelette—usually a potato omelette. When served as a tapa, the tortilla is cut into squares or wedges and served at room temperature.

1/2 cup extra-virgin olive oil
1 pound baking potatoes (about 2 large), peeled and thinly sliced
1 small yellow onion, diced
5 large eggs
Salt to taste

Heat oil in a heavy skillet. Add potatoes and onion, and season with salt. Cover and cook, but DO NOT allow potatoes to become crisp or brown.

In a large bowl, beat eggs with a fork. With a slotted spoon, add potatoes and onions, and stir until well coated. Add salt to taste.

Drain most of the oil from the skillet, leaving about 1 tablespoon. Place egg-and-potato mixture in skillet and cook until golden. Place a plate on top of the omelette and flip it over, so that the uncooked side is down, and slide it back into the pan. Cook until firm. Cut into squares to serve.

Prep time: 30 minutes
Yield: 6 to 8 tapas portions

Shrimp with Garlic

Shrimp in various guises are common on the tapas table.

6 tablespoons extra-virgin olive oil
6 cloves garlic, peeled and sliced
1 pound medium shrimp, peeled and deveined
1 dried red chili pepper, seeded and crushed
Salt to taste

In a heavy skillet, sauté garlic in the oil until golden but not brown. Add shrimp and chili. Cover and cook until done, about 4 minutes. Season with salt.

Prep time: 15 minutes
Yield: Serves 4-6 as tapas

Roasted Asparagus

Steamed asparagus is good; roasted asparagus is wonderful.

1 tablespoon garlic, minced
1 pound fresh asparagus, washed and trimmed
1 tablespoon olive oil
1 tablespoon red wine vinegar
Salt and freshly ground pepper to taste
1/2 cup dry bread crumbs
Pinch red pepper flakes
2 tablespoons almonds, toasted and chopped

Preheat oven to 500°F. Place garlic in an ovenproof skillet and roast until slightly browned. Remove garlic and set aside.

Add asparagus to the skillet, coating it evenly with the oil. Roast until tender-crunchy, about 5 minutes.

Combine asparagus and garlic on a serving platter and drizzle with vinegar, salt, and pepper.

Add bread crumbs, red pepper flakes, and almonds to the skillet and return to oven for several minutes to brown. Remove crumbs from oven and sprinkle over the asparagus. Roll asparagus to completely coat in bread crumbs.

Prep time: 20 minutes
Yield: 6 servings

WHERE THE NUTS COME FROM

Spain and Italy are the leading exporters of pine nuts: piñones *in Spain,* pignolias *in Italy.*

THE SHADY PAST
OF THE TOMATO

■

*A member of the night-
shade family, the tomato
has had to live down such
disreputable relatives as
jimsonweed (a hallucino-
gen), tobacco, and night-
shade itself, a legendary
poison used for centuries
to dispatch one's most
unsavory enemies.*

*Indigenous to the Andes
and domesticated in Mexico,
the tomato was ferried back
to Spain after the conquest
of Mexico. While it spread
rather quickly to the rest
of Europe, it was considered
a deadly poison and was*

Tomato and Anchovy Tart

In the tapas bars of Catalonia and the Basque provinces, fried fresh anchovies are a staple item. While fresh anchovies may not be widely available, canned ones will do nicely in this typically Spanish dish.

1 sheet puff pastry
1 teaspoon olive oil
5 cloves garlic, minced
1 cup sofrito (see the recipe on page 109)
1 tablespoon fresh rosemary
3 plum tomatoes, thinly sliced
4 anchovy filets, rinsed, dried, and chopped
1/2 cup grated parmesan
Sprigs of fresh rosemary

Preheat oven to 425°F. On a lightly floured surface, roll the puff pastry dough into a 13-inch circle. Place pastry in a very lightly greased and floured tart tin with removable rim. Trim excess dough from around the edges and place the crust in the freezer until ready to use.

Heat the oil in a cast-iron skillet over medium heat. Add garlic and sauté until soft. Reduce the heat to low and add sofrito and chopped rosemary. Simmer briefly and allow to cool completely.

While the shell is still frozen, spread sofrito mixture over bottom of the tart, covering it completely. Place tomato slices on the sofrito, then add the chopped anchovies, distributing both evenly. Sprinkle parmesan cheese over the top.

Bake the tart until golden brown and crispy, about 20 to 25 minutes. Garnish with sprigs of fresh rosemary.

Prep and cooking time: 40 minutes
Yield: 8 servings

Sofrito

Sofrito is the foundation of a multitude of Spanish dishes.

2 15-ounce cans tomatoes, seeded and chopped
3 tablespoons olive oil
3 cups chopped onion

Drain tomatoes thoroughly. Heat the oil in a deep, heavy pot over medium heat. Add the onion, reduce the heat, and simmer, covered, until onion is very soft, stirring occasionally. Add tomatoes and cook until the liquid is evaporated (about 1 hour).

Store sofrito in the refrigerator.

Prep time: 10 minutes
Cooking time: 1 hour
Yield: 3 cups

Savory Olive Spread

1 cup fresh basil leaves, packed
1 cup fresh spinach leaves, packed
1/2 cup pitted Kalamata olives
6 cloves garlic, crushed
3 tablespoons freshly squeezed lemon juice
2 tablespoons virgin olive oil, or slightly more if necessary to smooth

In a food processor or blender, puree all ingredients except the olive oil to a coarse paste. With the motor running, add the olive oil gradually. Refrigerate until ready to serve.

Serve with toasted slices of bread or with crackers.

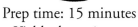

Prep time: 15 minutes
Yield: about 1 cup

cultivated only as an ornamental. (The English christened it, perhaps ironically, the "love apple.") For centuries, only the Italians could summon the nerve to eat it. In North America it was viewed with suspicion up to the turn of the century.

Now, of course, it's the most widely home-grown vegetable in the Western world, and it would be difficult to name a cuisine that would not be impoverished by its loss.

Tomato Tidbits

■ *Storing tomatoes in the refrigerator stops the ripening process. They'll do better in a cool, dry place.*

■ *The quickest way to seed a tomato is to cut it crosswise, exposing all the seed pockets, then squeeze it gently to force the seeds out.*

■ *To peel a tomato, immerse it for 15 to 30 seconds in boiling water. The skin slips right off. This works especially well with tomatoes intended for cooked dishes.*

■ *If the tomato is especially juicy, parboiling it before peeling can make it watery. An alternative is to core the tomato, pierce it with a fork, and hold it over a gas flame for a few seconds, rotating it until the skin loosens on all sides.*

Romesco Sauce

This truly wonderful salsa is named for the small red peppers that flavor it. An excellent accompaniment to fish and meat dishes, it makes an equally successful dip for vegetables and a fine spread for crackers or bread.

3 dried mild red chilies
4 tablespoons olive oil, preferably a strong-flavored Spanish variety, divided
5 tablespoons almonds or hazelnuts, blanched and chopped
6 slices 1/2-inch-thick French bread, crusts removed
6 cloves garlic, crushed
3 medium tomatoes, peeled, seeded, and chopped
1 tablespoon red wine vinegar
1 teaspoon sweet paprika
Pinch salt
Freshly ground pepper

Stem and seed the chilies, and soak them in 2 cups boiling water for 30 minutes.

Place 2 tablespoons of the oil in a heavy skillet, add the almonds, and cook over moderate heat until golden, stirring occasionally. With a slotted spoon, transfer almonds to a paper towel to drain.

In the same skillet, on moderately high heat, sauté the bread on both sides until crisp and brown, adding more oil as necessary. Transfer the bread to drain on a paper towel.

Remove the softened chiles from the water and pat dry. Sauté them briefly in the same skillet.

In a food processor or blender, puree the almonds with the garlic. Add the toasted bread, tomatoes, and vinegar, and puree. With the machine running, slowly add the remaining oil. Season with paprika, salt, and pepper.

The sauce will keep for about 1 week, covered and refrigerated.

Prep time: 30 minutes
Yield: about 1-1/2 cups.

Batter-Fried Scallions

1 large egg
1 cup water
1-1/2 cups all-purpose flour (divided)
1 teaspoon freshly grated parmesan
1 clove garlic, minced
1 teaspoon fresh parsley, minced
Pinch sweet paprika
1/2 teaspoon baking powder
Salt and pepper to taste
4 bunches scallions,
*   whites with 1 inch green top*
Vegetable oil for frying

In a food processor or blender, combine the egg, water, 1-1/4 cups flour, cheese, garlic, parsley, paprika, and baking powder. Process until a light batter is formed.

Place the remaining 1/4 cup flour in a medium bowl, and add salt and pepper to taste.

Heat the vegetable oil to medium (350°F). Working a handful at a time, dredge the scallions in the flour. Shake off the excess flour, dip the onions into the batter, and fry in the oil for 4 minutes, or until golden. Transfer to paper towels to drain.

Prep time: 30 minutes
Yield: about 40 scallions

Banderillas

Named for the well-decorated darts used in the Spanish bullring, banderillas are bits of food skewered on oversize toothpicks or small wooden skewers. Fun to eat and easy to prepare, they can be put together in a spur-of-the-moment fashion or planned for with more care.

Try to alternate ingredients to vary the color, texture, and taste—a sweet pearl onion followed by a salty anchovy followed by a fresh red pepper, for example. Although you can use any tidbits you want, here are some common ones:

Green Spanish olive, plain or marinated (see recipe on page 105)
Cube of marinated potato (see recipe on page 113)
Rolled anchovy, with or without caper
1/2-inch crosswise slice of sweet or dill pickle
Chunk of white meat tuna
1-inch length of roasted asparagus (see recipe on page 107)
1-inch crosswise slice of hard-boiled egg
Half a marinated artichoke
Slice of chorizo

Marinated Onions

These can be served alone or speared on skewers for banderillas.

1 small onion, chopped
1 clove garlic, minced
2 tablespoons olive oil
1 medium tomato, peeled, seeded, and chopped
1 tablespoon finely chopped parsley
1 bay leaf
1/4 teaspoon thyme

1/2 teaspoon basil
Salt and pepper to taste
1/2 pound pearl onions, peeled
1/4 cup white vine vinegar
2 tablespoons raisins
1 tablespoon sugar

Sauté the chopped onion and garlic in the olive oil until transparent. Add tomato, parsley, bay leaf, thyme, basil, salt, and pepper, and simmer 5 to 10 minutes. Add remaining ingredients plus 1/2 cup water, and simmer for 30 to 40 minutes. Let cool and refrigerate for 1 or 2 hours before serving.

Prep time: 30 minutes
Cooking time: 1 hour
Rest time: 1 to 2 hours
Yield: 8 servings

Potatoes with Capers and Dill

These potatoes are delicious alone or excellent on banderillas.

1-1/2 pounds potatoes (about 3 medium), preferably red waxy
1/3 cup olive oil
2 tablespoons fresh lemon juice
3 tablespoons fresh orange juice
1/2 small onion, finely chopped
2 tablespoons minced parsley
1 tablespoon minced fresh dill
1-1/2 tablespoons small capers
Salt and pepper

Boil potatoes in their skins until done, being careful not to overcook into mushiness. Drain the potatoes and run them under cold water to stop the cooking. If you're using red waxy or other thin-skinned potatoes, leave them unpeeled; otherwise, peel them. Cut into 3/4-inch cubes and set aside.

Stir together remaining ingredients and pour the dressing over the potatoes. Marinate at room temperature for several hours.

Prep time: 20 minutes
Cooking time: 30 minutes
Marinating time: 2 hours

CAPERS

Capers are the tight little flower buds of a spindly shrub found in the Mediterranean region. Produced largely in Spain, Italy, and Algeria, capers are picked in early summer and pickled in vinegar. Salty, mildly pungent, somewhat reminiscent of olives but less intrusive, capers enliven bland dishes and complement rice, potatoes, and eggs especially well. Given a choice, buy jars of very small capers; the large ones are often nasturtium buds anyway. Rinse capers before using them, to remove excess preserving salt.

United States

Although some would argue that this nation of immigrants has no identifiable cuisine, in fact we do. As Senator S.I. Hayakawa said of the Panama Canal, "We stole it fair and square."

Like its people, the food of the United States has been assembled from the four corners of the globe. When immigrants arrived from Europe, Asia, Africa, and the Middle East, they brought with them their styles of cooking, their lists of preferred ingredients, and their notions of what tasted good and what did not. The result has been a hyphenated cuisine of enormous richness and diversity: Italian-American, Chinese-American, Indian-American, Polish-American, Mexican-American, Jamaican-American, and so on.

Like every other cuisine, American food has been defined by the foods available. Immigrants adapted their recipes, doing without the ingredients they couldn't find, adding new ones that seemed to serve almost as well. The result has been such hybrids as stir-fried broccoli and peach salsa.

There are pockets of absolutely unique ways of eating. In Louisiana, Cajun cooking combines a French-Canadian heritage with African elements to produce a fiery food. (Cajun spice mixtures often use black, red, *and* white ground peppers.) On the shores of Chesapeake Bay, which until recently was unrivaled

in its production of shellfish, Maryland crab cakes became an internationally applauded dish. Profoundly influenced by the African slaves who did much of the work, Southern cooking contributed much to the national fare, including an addiction to ham biscuits.

But American cuisine has come mostly from Americans' ability to recognize a good thing when they saw it. When G.I.'s returned from Europe after World War II, they brought home a passion for Italian food, and pizza became a national obsession. Yankee tourists in Switzerland fell in love with fondue, and Americans have been dipping bread in melted cheese ever since.

Then there's the much-ballyhooed "American enterprise." A bartender in Buffalo, New York, figured out that his customers would drink more beer if they were thirsty, and he gave us buffalo wings—bite-size pieces of chicken marinated in a hot, spicy sauce.

Eclectic, adventurous, cheerfully inconsistent, American food is notable for its capacity to experiment with familiar foods and flavors, combining and transforming them into something new.

Cajun Sweet Potato Chips

The sweetness of the potatoes contrasts nicely with the hot Cajun spices.

1 tablespoon paprika
2-1/2 teaspoons salt
1 teaspoon onion powder
1 teaspoon garlic powder
1 teaspoon cayenne

3/4 teaspoon white pepper
3/4 teaspoon black pepper
2 to 4 sweet potatoes, peeled
Vegetable oil for deep frying

Combine the spices and mix well. Set aside.

Peel the sweet potatoes and cut off the ends. Using a vegetable peeler with a wide blade, shave a very thin strip from the length of the potato. If you don't have a wide peeler, use a very sharp knife. The thinner the strips, the crisper the chips.

Heat the oil to medium hot (350°F) and deep-fry the chips until crisp—a few seconds for very thin chips, a couple of minutes for thicker slices. Do not allow them to brown. Set the chips on several layers of paper towels to drain. While the chips are still hot, sprinkle them with the spice mixture.

Prep and cooking time: 20 minutes
Yield: 8 servings

(SEA) SALT AND (FRESHLY GROUND) PEPPER

In any group of good cooks, you can start an argument almost at will by suggesting that, compared to ordinary table salt, sea salt is saltier, more flavorful, and even more healthful, because of its trace minerals. On this issue, we vote for the ocean. Although sea salt costs a little more loose change, we think it really does taste better and is thus worth finding and using.

On the other hand, as a trouble-making issue, black pepper is a dud. Any food

116

Boiled Peanuts

From July to October, back roads in the Southern United States are dotted with hand-lettered signs that yell, "Boiled Peanuts!" Next to the sign is a ramshackle frame building, and next to that is a huge iron pot steaming over a wood fire. Lured by the irresistible smell of hot peanuts, passing motorists screech to a halt, then drive off with brown paper bags full of hot, wet peanuts, trying desperately to eat them before they cool or soak through the bottom of the bag.

8 cups unshelled green peanuts, preferably the small Valencias
3 tablespoons salt
3 quarts water

In a huge pot or soup kettle, bring the salted water to a low boil. Add peanuts and cook for 1 to 2 hours. Leave the peanuts in the bath until they are as salty as you like them. Serve hot with lots of paper towels.

Cooking time: 1 to 2 hours
Yield: 8 cups

Garden Pizzas with Fresh Tomatoes

Americans are constantly thinking up new toppings for pizza—including this combination of creamy goat cheese, sweet tomatoes, and spicy vinaigrette. Be sure to remove all the pulpy seeds from the tomatoes, or the pizzas will be soggy.

The crust:
1 cup warm water
1 tablespoon dry active yeast
1 tablespoon sugar
1 tablespoon virgin olive oil
2-1/2 to 3 cups all-purpose flour

lover will vote for grinding your own. Some will maintain that canned, commercially ground pepper should be a controlled substance, available only under a physician's care.

COUNTING SHRIMP

In a mixing bowl, combine the warm water and the yeast. Allow to stand for a minute. Stir in the sugar, olive oil, and 1-1/2 cups of the flour, mixing thoroughly.

Gradually stir in the rest of the flour. Turn the dough onto a lightly floured board. Knead until the dough is smooth and elastic, about 5 minutes.

Shape the dough into a ball, place it in a well-oiled bowl, and cover with a towel or plastic wrap. Set in a warm spot and allow to rise for 1 hour.

Punch dough down. Using a rolling pin, roll the dough to a thickness of 1/4 inch. Using a large round cookie cutter or bowl rim, cut 8 rounds from the dough about 4 to 5 inches in diameter.

Place the pizza shells on a dark baking sheet or pizza stone that has been lightly oiled and dusted with cornmeal.

The dressing:
2 shallots, minced
1 tablespoon Dijon mustard
2 tablespoons balsamic vinegar
6 tablespoons extra-virgin olive oil
Pinch of salt

Combine the shallots, mustard, and vinegar in a bowl. Gradually add the oil in a thin stream, whisking constantly, until the dressing is thick and emulsified. Whisk in salt.

The topping:
4 to 6 tablespoons milk or cream
12 ounces mild goat cheese
3 ripe tomatoes, seeded and chopped
8 sun-dried tomatoes, chopped
16 large fresh basil leaves, chopped
Freshly ground black pepper

Stir the milk or cream into the cheese, adding only enough liquid to make a thick spreading consistency. Set aside with remaining topping ingredients.

Assembly:

Preheat oven to 500°F. The oven must be extremely hot, so make sure to preheat completely.

With a basting brush, brush the pizza crusts liberally with the dressing. Spread each with the cheese mixture. Sprinkle the remaining topping ingredients over the cheese, then dribble more dressing on top, saving the freshly ground black pepper until last.

Place the pizzas on the lowest rack in the oven and immediately reduce the heat to 450°F. Bake 12 to 15 minutes, or until the crust is done.

Prep time: 45 minutes, plus 1 hour rising time.
Yield: 8 servings

Scallion Biscuits with Honey Ham and Fruit Salsa

Many an American starts the day with a ham biscuit.

The biscuits:

2-1/2 cups all-purpose flour
4 teaspoons baking powder
1 teaspoon salt
2 tablespoons sugar
3 tablespoons chopped scallions, both green and white parts
7 tablespoons chilled butter, cut into small pieces
1 cup buttermilk, divided
1 large egg

Preheat the oven to 375°F.

STORING FRESH HERBS

■

Picked fresh herbs will keep for days if you treat them like cut fresh flowers. Trim the bottom of the stems and place the herbs in a glass of water. Set them on a counter top, if you like; an herb bouquet does wonders for the disposition. For maximum keeping power, cover the foliage loosely with a plastic bag and store the whole arrangement— glass, water, herbs, and bag— in the refrigerator.

SMOKING FISH

A small, stove-top smoker is available for the home cook, making it possible to smoke small amounts of food without investing in one of the larger models. It is shaped like a cake pan with a sliding lid and an interior rack.

To use one, follow the manufacturer's instructions carefully. Usually, you'll select the hardwood chips of your choice—hickory, mesquite, oak, apple—and soak them in water for 1 hour. Cover the bottom of the smoker with wet chips, adding enough water to barely cover the bottom of the pan. Return the rack to the smoker and arrange the food on the rack. Close the lid and set the smoker on the stove over medium heat. As the chips heat, they will begin to smoke. Watch carefully and add water if the pan starts to scorch. The fish is done when it turns opaque and is easily pierced with a fork.

In a large bowl, combine the flour, baking powder, salt, and sugar. Stir in the scaliions. Using a pastry fork or two sharp knives, cut in the butter until the mixture resembles coarse meal.

In a separate bowl, mix together 3/4 cup of the buttermilk and the egg. Add to the dry mix and stir quickly just until the liquid is incorporated, being careful not to overmix.

Turn the dough onto a well-floured surface and pat it to a thickness of 3/4 inch. Using a cookie cutter about 2 inches in diameter, cut rounds from the dough and place them on a baking sheet that has been lightly oiled and dusted with cornmeal. Let the biscuits touch each other. Brush the tops of the biscuits with the reserved buttermilk.

Bake for about 20 minutes, or until golden. Place on a rack to cool.

The salsa:
1 cup coarsely chopped fresh peaches, mangos,
*   or pineapple, or a combination*
1 tablespoon chopped scallions
1 tablespoon chopped jalapeño pepper
1 tablespoon chopped anaheim pepper,
*   or other mild pepper*
1 teaspoon fresh lime zest
Salt and pepper to taste

Combine all ingredients.

Assembly:
1/4 pound thinly sliced honey-baked ham divided into 16 portions

Slice the biscuits in half. Place a portion of ham on the bottom half of each biscuit and top with 1 tablespoon salsa. Add the tops of the biscuits and serve.

Prep time: 1 hour
Yield: 16 biscuits

Smokies

This dish is named for the Great Smoky Mountains in the southern part of the country, where the streams are alive with native trout. It is outstanding.

1 pound smoked trout,
* broken into chunks (see "Smoking Fish")*
1 cup grated cheddar cheese
1 cup grated Monterey jack cheese

1 cup heavy cream or half-and-half
Fresh tomato salsa (see recipe below)
Tortilla chips or crackers

Preheat oven to 450°F.

Divide the smoked trout among 8 individual oiled ramekins, or place it in a large, shallow baking dish. Divide both cheeses into 8 portions and sprinkle over the trout. Place a generous dollop of salsa on top, then pour in the cream or half-and-half.

Bake until bubbling hot and golden, about 10 minutes. Serve hot with tortilla chips or crackers.

Prep time: 30 minutes
Yield: 8 servings

Tomato Salsa

4 small, ripe tomatoes, seeded and chopped
4 tomatillos, chopped
1 tablespoon minced jalapeño pepper
2 tablespoons minced anaheim pepper
* (or other mild pepper)*

2 teaspoons chopped scallions
2 teaspoons freshly squeezed lemon juice
1/2 teaspoon roasted cumin seeds, ground
* (see "Roasting Spices," page 100)*
Sprinkling of garlic powder

Combine all ingredients.

COOKING QUICKLY

■

Sometimes the methodical tasks of cooking are welcome relaxation. On the other hand, if we can cook quickly when we want to, we increase the number of dishes we can make when time is limited.

1. *Get some labor- and time-saving tools: a blender, food processor, spice grinder, and whatever chopping/mincing/shredding tools work for you. Ask your friends and fellow cooks what really works and what is just a pointless gadget.*

2. *Razor-sharp knives are incredibly useful time-savers and boredom-reducers.*

121

Unless they've been sharpened recently, they're probably working at a fraction of their potential.

3. *Keep your pantry stocked with condiments and basic ingredients. Make a master list of the items you use constantly—wine vinegar? tomato sauce? olive oil?—and post it on your pantry wall. Check the list before major shopping trips and resupply as necessary.*

4. *Always read through a recipe at least twice before you begin to cook. Visualize the process. Think through the recipe, mentally dividing the individual steps into major operations. Get an overall sense of the logic of the recipe.*

5. *Prepare all your ingredients beforehand; chop everything that must be chopped*

Buffalo Wings with Blue Cheese Dip

Serve these fiery wings with lots of cold beer or iced tea. The cooling cheese dip is optional. We've deep-fried the wings, but they can be roasted or grilled, if you prefer.

1/4 cup Tabasco sauce, plus 2 tablespoons (divided)
1 tablespoon Worcestershire sauce
4 pounds chicken wings
Vegetable oil for deep-frying
3 tablespoons unsalted butter

In a large mixing bowl, combine the 1/4 cup Tabasco and the Worcestershire sauce. Add the wings and turn to coat. Marinate overnight in the refrigerator.

Heat the vegetable oil to medium hot (375°F) and deep-fry the wings until done, about 5 minutes. (When done, they should float to the surface.) Remove and drain immediately on paper towels. Transfer to a platter.

In a small saucepan, combine the 2 tablespoons of Tabasco with the butter. Heat until butter is melted and sauce is bubbly. Toss the wings with the butter sauce. Serve with Creamy Cheese Dip and celery sticks.

Creamy Cheese Dip

2/3 cup sour cream
1/3 cup mayonnaise
4 tablespoons minced celery
1 tablespoon minced scallions

1/4 pound crumbled blue cheese
Dash of Worcestershire sauce
Several drops Tabasco
Salt and pepper to taste

Combine all ingredients. Store in the refrigerator.

Stuffed Baby Vegetables

It's hard to say why Americans are so captivated by miniature vegetables. Perhaps they simply look like toys. Good candidates for stuffing include miniature zucchini, patty-pan squash, and eggplant.

36 assorted miniature vegetables
1 cup diced vegetable from middle
*   of baby vegetables*
1/2 medium onion, diced
2 tablespoons extra-virgin olive oil
4 cloves garlic, minced
Salt and freshly ground pepper to taste
1/2 pound mushrooms, finely chopped
1/4 cup dry white wine
2 sun-dried tomatoes packed in oil,
*   drained and diced*
2 tablespoons pine nuts,
*   toasted and chopped*
1/3 cup grated parmesan cheese
2 tablespoons chopped parsley

The vegetables:

Wash the vegetables. Cut off the top one-third of each vegetable. (The location of the cut will depend on the shape of the vegetable.) Don't discard the tops.

Using a melon baller, a sharp paring knife, and/or a serrated grapefruit spoon, scoop out much of the inside of each vegetable, leaving a wall at least 1/4 inch thick. Reserve the scooped-out parts of the vegetable. Sprinkle the inside of the vegetable shells with salt.

Steam the vegetable shells and their tops briefly, just until tender crisp. Vegetables must remain firm. Check frequently, being careful not to overcook into mushiness.

The filling:

Chop the reserved scooped-out centers of the vegetables, discarding any seeds or strings, to make 1 cup.

6. *Find the pattern that makes utensils quick and easy for you to find. Some cooks organize by type of tool (all their wooden spoons upright in one tool pot). Other cooks organize by frequency of use, keeping a container of the tools they work with constantly close at hand, no matter how dissimilar the tools are to each other.*

In a large skillet, sauté the onion in the olive oil until translucent. Add garlic and diced vegetables. Season with salt and pepper and cook until tender. Add mushrooms and cook 1 minute more. Add white wine and simmer until almost dry. Remove pan from heat.

Stir in the sun-dried tomatoes and pine nuts, plus half the parmesan and half the parsley. Toss to combine.

Stuff the vegetables with the filling. Place the filled vegetables in a lightly oiled baking dish. Sprinkle with the remaining parmesan and bake, uncovered, for 5 minutes. Remove from oven and sprinkle with reserved parsley. Replace the vegetable tops and serve.

Prep time: 1 hour
Yield: 36 vegetables

Cheese Fondue

Fondue is a friendly dish, encouraging good conversation and occasional hilarity as people jockey for position around the fondue pot. It's good party fare. If you have trouble locating any of the cheeses listed below, just substitute ordinary Swiss.

1 clove garlic, peeled and halved lengthwise
2 cups dry white wine
1-1/2 tablespoons flour
1/2 pound Emmanthaler, shredded
1/2 pound Gruyère, shredded
1/8 pound Appenzeller, shredded (optional)

3 tablespoons kirsch
Sprinkling of nutmeg
Cracked black pepper to taste
Day-old French bread,
*   cut into 1-inch cubes*
Tart apple wedges

The easiest fondues are accomplished with electric fondue pots, which are widely available and relatively inexpensive. You can also use a round, heatproof chafing dish with great success.

Rub the insides of the fondue pot or chafing dish with the garlic, then discard the garlic. Pour in the wine and heat to a simmer (on the stovetop, if you're using a chafing dish).

Sprinkle the flour over the grated cheese and toss to coat. Keeping the wine at low heat, add the cheese a handful at a time. Use a wooden spoon to stir in a figure-eight motion after each addition until the cheese is melted. Add the kirsch. Season with the nutmeg and pepper.

To serve, transfer the dish from the stovetop to the chafer bottom to maintain heat. Pierce the bread cubes and apple wedges with skewers or fondue forks and dunk into the hot cheese mixture, occasionally stirring in a figure-eight motion.

The crust that will form on the bottom of the dish is highly prized, known reverently as "la réligieuse."

Prep time: 45 minutes
Yield: 4 servings

Crab Cakes with Dill Mayonnaise

A legacy of the Maryland shore, crab cakes are among America's best-loved finger foods.

2 pounds crabmeat, preferably
  blue lump, claw, or a combination
3 eggs
1 tablespoon Dijon mustard
1 tablespoon lemon juice
4 tablespoons light virgin olive oil
1/2 teaspoon dried thyme
1/2 teaspoon salt
1/2 teaspoon freshly ground black pepper
1/8 teaspoon cayenne
3 celery stalks, minced
1 medium sweet red onion, chopped fine
1-1/4 waxed-paper "sleeves" of saltine crackers
    (they come 4 to a 1-pound box), coarsely crumbled
1 to 2 tablespoons vegetable oil
Sprigs of fresh dill and lemon wedges (to garnish)

125

Pick over the crabmeat to remove any shell pieces. Drain well.

Combine all ingredients in a large bowl and mix well. If the mixture is too wet to mold into a patty, add extra cracker crumbs. If too dry, add a little more oil.

Form the crab mixture into cakes about 2 inches in diameter and 1 inch high. Sauté in the vegetable oil over medium heat until cooked through.

Serve with a dollop of Dill Mayonnaise. Garnish with a sprig of fresh dill.

Prep time: 1 hour
Yield: 6 to 8 servings

Dill Mayonnaise

1-1/2 cups mayonnaise
2 teaspoons minced fresh dill
3 scallions, minced

Combine all ingredients and mix thoroughly. Store in refrigerator.